"Tired? Exhausted? Worn out? At last, real help is here. Stephens and Gray will help you climb out of the "worn out" trap so you can be all God wants you to be. Full of truth, joy, and hope, this book is sprinkled with down-to-earth practical tips and will encourage any woman who feels at the end of her rope!"

"If you're running on fumes, this very insightful guidebook is for you! My friends Dr. Steve and Alice will lead you step-by-step to that joy-filled place called balance."

"Hope for the worn-out woman...I want some—I *got* some! Dr. Steve Stephens and Alice Gray have teamed up to write a book that hit a home run of hope to my heart! If you are sick and tired of being sick and tired, or you want to avoid feeling that way, then this book is definitely for you!"

"Just a few pages into this book and I knew I'd found something very special! Alice Gray and Dr. Steve Stephens have created an oasis for *The Worn Out Woman,* an off-ramp on the busy high-way of life. Taken in little sips or long, deeply drunk draughts, you'll find refreshing water for your soul as well as new strength and direction to face every day. This is a book you'll read over and over—one you'll want to share with a friend!"

the worn out woman

the worn out woman

Dr. Steve Stephens & Alice Gray

Multnomah® Publishers *Sisters, Oregon*

THE WORN OUT WOMAN
published by Multnomah Publishers, Inc.
© 2004 by Steve Stephens and Alice Gray
International Standard Book Number: 1-59052-266-4

Cover design by Steve Gardner, His Image PixelWorks
Cover and selected interior images by Steve Gardner, His Image PixelWorks

Unless otherwise indicated, Scripture quotations are from:
Holy Bible, New Living Translation
© 1996. Used by permission of Tyndale House Publishers, Inc.
All rights reserved.

Other Scripture quotations are from:
The Holy Bible, New International Version (NIV) © 1973, 1984 by
International Bible Society, used by permission of Zondervan Publishing House.
New American Standard Bible® (NASB) © 1960, 1977, 1995
by the Lockman Foundation. Used by permission.
The New Testament in Modern English, Revised Edition (Phillips)
© 1958, 1960, 1972 by J. B. Phillips
The Living Bible (TLB) © 1971.
Used by permission of Tyndale House Publishers, Inc.
All rights reserved.
The Holy Bible, New King James Version (NKJV)
© 1984 by Thomas Nelson, Inc.
The Message, © 1993, 1994, 1995, 1996, 2000, 2001, 2002
Used by permission of NavPress Publishing Group

Multnomah is a trademark of Multnomah Publishers, Inc.,
and is registered in the U.S. Patent and Trademark Office.
The colophon is a trademark of Multnomah Publishers, Inc.
Printed in the United States of America

For information:
MULTNOMAH PUBLISHERS, INC.
POST OFFICE BOX 1720
SISTERS, OREGON 97759

04 05 06 07 08 09 10—10 9 8 7 6 5 4 3

*To the women who
live to give God pleasure.
You are our inspiration.*

Contents

A Special Thank You to...

Our friends Allison Alison, Sandi Bottemiller, Anita Crowther, Carol Clifton, Jen Distler, Barb Majors, Bonnie Marston, Leslie Wait, and Marty Williams.

The thoughtful insights you gave after reading an early manuscript are sprinkled through every chapter.

Our trusted editor, Anne Christian Buchanan.

If books were like songs, you added the melody.

Our treasured life partners, Tami Stephens and Al Gray.

Your prayers and encouragement were daily gifts to us.

Our Lord and Savior, Jesus Christ.

We are grateful that You keep teaching us. Even though we have miles to go, we pray You will find pleasure in what we have written.

Note to Our Readers

We have used many true stories in this book. But unless we had specific permission from the women involved, we changed the names and altered the circumstances enough to protect their privacy.

Winter Night

I am worn to a raveling.

BEATRIX POTTER, *THE TAILOR OF GLOUCESTER*

ate one winter night, five women lingered in the fire-
side room of a popular retreat center. We chose a
cozy fireplace corner that was thoughtfully furnished
for comfort and conversation. The soothing glow of
burning embers, steaming mugs of hot chocolate,
and a satisfying fatigue after a day of meetings drew us
together. We curled our stockinged feet under us, snuggled
deeper into the soft cushions, and began a conversation
that would change the course of our lives.

When women get away from hectic schedules and daily
worries, it's fascinating how quickly we become intimate.
Intimate not only with God and our heart's desires, but also
with each other in honest conversation. Even though we
five had just met that afternoon, the retreat setting had
already spun its magic, and we were ready to talk like the
best of friends.

I (Alice) took a moment to study the group and smiled
at the unusual mosaic we made. Different ages, different
personalities, different circumstances. And yet we had

13

established an immediate camaraderie. The common thread that drew us together was a deep desire to be the kind of women God had in mind when He created us. But as we talked I began to see another commonality—the sense of being too worn out to pursue our passions.

Sometimes in a whisper, often with tears streaming down their cheeks, these women shared their weariness and frustration:

✔❋ Most days I feel overwhelmed.

✔❋ I want to run away and start over again.

❋ I've wished my life away.

✔❋ I hardly ever experience intimate or tender moments with the Lord.

❋ My days are filled with things I don't want to do.

❋ When I read the Bible, it's out of habit rather than desire.

❋ The joy and excitement are gone.

❋ I wake up feeling discouraged.

❋ I've taken on responsibilities that I never wanted.

✔❋ I feel like I'm missing me. But maybe it's God I'm missing.

As our sharing time drew to a close, I realized the women were looking to me for solutions. Because I was the conference speaker, they expected me to have answers for their two main questions: "How did I get this way?" and "Is there a way out?" I wanted to be helpful but knew I didn't have the final answer that would fully satisfy their heart longings.

Still, these women had been honest with me, and now it was my turn to be honest with them. So I told them that the feelings they shared echoed what was often in my own heart. Although I sincerely longed to be the woman God intended me to be and had made some progress in that area, at times my life still felt out of control and over-whelming. Each time I fell back into what I call "race-pace mode," I realized I had many more miles of learning. Like the women in that room, I was still looking for the life-changing treasure called balance.

Those women were wonderful to me that night. They seemed to love me more for my honesty than when they thought I had it all together. We held hands and prayed for each other and finally ended the evening with long hugs and whispered promises to find the answers that would change the pace of our lives.

Since then, it seems I've encountered more and more women who struggle with the issues we talked about that night. Most are energetic, accomplished women. They sincerely desire God's best for their lives. And yet they are exhausted, discouraged, burned out, missing joy. They know something is wrong, but they're not quite sure how to make it all right—and they're not sure they have the energy to try.

Sound familiar? You're not alone. The worn-out woman has many sisters. But there is abundant hope for any worn-out woman...so please read on!

15

Two months after the retreat, I happened to talk with my friend Dr. Steve Stephens, who mentioned his own concerns about women on overload and how it affects their marriages, children, careers, friendships, and intimacy with God. Steve is a Christian marriage and family therapist who, in twenty-five years of practice, has helped hundreds of women suffering the consequences of high-pressure living. Since then, Steve and I have worked together on a series of eight books called Lists to Live By. At the completion of each project, our conversation always seemed to return to our desire to help women find balance in their lives. Finally, after hours of discussion and prayer, we started this book—one we pray will give some answers that worn-out women are searching for.

In a way we are unusual writing partners, because our lives are so different—and yet we believe we each have something unique to contribute. Steve is a counseling professional who has seen positive—even dramatic—results in countless women who have followed his wise guidance. In addition to being a leader in the Christian community, Steve is greatly respected for his ability to counsel with a balance of grace and truth. Steve has been married to his loving wife, Tami, for twenty years. They live in Oregon and have three children. He is also a sought-after speaker for couple and family retreats.

I, on the other hand, am a woman who has lived what we are writing about (more on that later). I've also held various roles as a leader in women's ministries and enjoy speaking at conferences, Bible studies, and smaller groups like MOPS (Mothers of Preschoolers). Our kitchen table is often a place for safe conversation when women need someone to listen and care. My wonderful husband, Al, and I live in Arizona. We have been married for thirty-seven years and have two precious granddaughters. (Yes, I have pictures!)

Because we live in different states, Steve and I initially divided up the chapters and wrote on our own. Then we spent days on the phone pooling our ideas and experiences and rewriting the chapters together. Through this process, you, the reader, were constantly in our thoughts and prayers, and we structured this book very intentionally.

Because we know you're busy (why else would you be feeling worn out?), we've kept the chapters short and practical. Each can be read comfortably in one sitting and put into practice right away. We've even included a section at the end of each chapter that will help you remember the important principles and try them out. At the same time, we believe no one can unclutter her life without uncluttering her heart as well, so we've included material to help you dig a little deeper into *why* you might be feeling worn out. We've included chapters, in fact, for all areas of your life—emotional, mental, social, physical, and spiritual.

You can read this book straight through in the order we have arranged it—or, if you prefer, you can look at the table of contents and see which chapters you want to read first. We were only able to skim the surface on some topics, so if you want more information, we suggest you check out the recommended reading list at the back of the book.

> From now on, I am going to grab the good times with both arms. I am going to walk outside and feel the sun on my face and learn to laugh, really laugh again.
>
> Most of all, I'm going to take the love that comes my way and hold on to it for dear life. Sometimes we don't need new scenery, just new eyes.
>
> DAWN MILLER[1]

In all of this, we want to encourage and inspire you because we are convinced there is hope. No matter how stressed and overwhelmed you might feel, you can experience the fulfilling life God has planned for you. Even if you have been worn out for so long that you can't remember what it's like to relax and laugh and feel peace, you really can recapture those simple joys in your life.

And now we have skipped ahead in our thoughts, imagining how you will feel when you finish reading. It is our prayer that you will leave the questions of the winter night behind and begin living the answers of a glorious new day.

Something to Try

You can choose just one...

* Write several sentences describing what draws you to this book and how you hope it will help you.

* Review the statements the women made while sharing at the retreat. Circle the ones that most identify your feelings. What comments would you add to the list?

* Write down three things you have tried in the past to cope with feeling worn out. What was successful? What wasn't?

* Buy a small bag of confetti at a party shop and select a pretty glass container for your kitchen counter or desk. Each time you have a satisfying day (or each time you read a chapter of this book), put a little confetti in the jar. When the jar is full, celebrate! I like to throw the confetti in the air and leave it wherever it falls for a day or two. Just looking at it makes me feel happy.

1

What's Going On?

Don't ask me to relax;
it's my tension that's holding me together.

AUTHOR UNKNOWN

mommy, I don't feel good."

Little Susie did look pale. Instinctively her mother felt her forehead and it seemed warm. So Susie's mother took out the thermometer and checked her daughter's temperature. It was a simple procedure, but it provided important information.

In the same way, you might do well to do a quick check on your level of weariness—to take the "temperature" of your life to see just how worn out you are. In this fast-paced, hectic, squeeze-as-much-as-you-can-into-your-day world, <u>you might be more exhausted than you think</u>. Each of us has our limits and our breaking points. Get too close to them, and you put yourself at risk for any number of problems.

But you probably already know that. You don't need to be told that you are weary and stressed—you feel it every day. And you are not alone. Studies estimate that there are more than sixty million worn-out women in the United States and that another sixty million are on the fast track to becoming exhausted and overwhelmed.

As I (Steve) counsel women about their lives and concerns, I am amazed at all they are trying to balance—caring for children; fixing meals; cleaning; decorating and maintaining their homes; volunteering at school, church, and community activities; hosting get-togethers; balancing finances; working at full-time or part-time jobs; loving their husbands; caring for aging parents; and seeing to all the other aspects of their daily lives.

I worry that many women are working at 120 percent of their capacity and feeling guilty because they are not doing more. That's probably true of you as well. You take what you do seriously and try to do the best you can. I know how responsible, caring, diligent, and active you are, but your life is so busy that you run out of energy long before the day is over.

Dear worn-out woman, you can't do it all, nor do you have to!

Have you ever felt that even though you're taking things "one day at a time"...it's about twenty-four more hours than you can take?

AUTHOR UNKNOWN

How Much Is Too Much?

The women who come to me for counseling certainly know they are feeling worn out, but many aren't sure what their symptoms mean and how serious they might be. They wonder if they are just too sensitive, if they have PMS, if they are experiencing the beginning of menopause, or if they're just "going through a phase." But even if part of their distress is due to hormonal or season-of-life issues, I usually find they are coping with long-term overload as well.

So how do you know when too much is too much? Chances are your body and mind have been trying to tell you, but you may be moving too fast to even notice. Or maybe you have gotten so accustomed to feeling worn out that exhaustion seems normal. You can't even imagine what it would feel like to have vitality and extra energy.

If you have even an inkling that being worn out might be an issue for you, then I urge you to take the little quiz on pages 24–25. The quiz lists eighteen symptoms of overload. Even one can signal a problem, but the more you have, the greater your risk. After marking your symptoms, slow down and consider what might lie behind your answers. Determine if these issues are constant or if they come and go. When do they surface, and what is involved when they do?

If you routinely experience more than three of the eighteen basic warning signs, it's time to make some changes. Try not to dismiss your results with statements like, "This is just the way life is" or "I'm not doing that badly." If you find it hard to evaluate yourself, a great way to double-check is to have a caring friend take the survey for you and point out the signs they see in your life.

Are You a Worn-out Woman?

The quiz below will help you "take the temperature" of your life when it comes to stressful overload. Read through the list carefully, and check off each item you have experienced more than once in the past week.

Add up your check marks for a quick assessment of how worn out you are right now, and evaluate your "score" according to the key at the end of the quiz.

☒ You get irritable or impatient over little things.

☒ You have a hard time getting to sleep or staying asleep.

❏ You seem overly emotional.

❏ Your body sometimes feels so wound up that you can't relax.

☒ You think, *If I can just get through this, then I'm going to do some of the things I really want to do.*

❏ You get frustrated at how forgetful you are.

☒ You are easily distracted, even from things you enjoy.

❏ Your friends say you are moody.

❏ You run out of energy before your day is done.

❏ You find it hard to make definite decisions or to stick to them once they are made.

☒ You get fed up when things take longer than you plan.

❏ You find yourself eating when you really aren't hungry.

❏ You avoid spending time with family or friends because they just take too much energy.

❏ You feel like nothing sounds fun or exciting.

❏ You enjoy the adrenaline rush of last-minute deadlines.

✗ You are not working up to your normal ability.

❑ You find that worry distracts you from reaching your goals.

❑ You have trouble delegating tasks because you think you can do them better.

If you checked... Your stress level is probably...

$\lbrack$ *1–6*   *Mild to moderate—be careful.*

$\lbrack$ *7–12*   *Serious—may need to make some changes.*

   13–18   *Severe—get help now!*

A Reason to Hope

When I speak with women's groups and share my little quiz, women come to me and say, "I thought I was doing pretty well, but now I really feel worn out and stressed."

My response, "That's great," usually catches them by surprise.

"That's great," I continue, "because now there is hope."

As long as you deny, ignore, or minimize these symptoms, you are headed for trouble. Even a mild to moderate level is a signal that something is not right. The higher your score, the greater the probability that you will face serious consequences. If you don't do something to change, you can easily end up with health problems, broken relationships, severe depression, or a number of other difficult consequences.

But don't panic! There is hope for the worn-out woman, but you have to take action. You have to *do* something.

The sad truth is that problems in our lives rarely get better by themselves. If you get a sliver in your thumb and ignore it, what happens? I suppose there is a slight chance the sliver will work its way out, but more likely the thumb will get infected. It turns red and hurts. In time it swells and throbs. The infection spreads, and if left untreated it even has the potential to kill you. But if you take the time to remove the splinter and perhaps apply an antibiotic, your thumb will probably be well in a day or two.

It's relatively simple to care for an infected thumb, but caring for your worn-out body, mind, and spirit can be trickier. You may know you need to do something but feel too tired or frustrated to do anything at all.

If that's true for you, consider that you've already taken the first step toward change, which is recognizing that you have a problem. With God's help and the support of those who love you, you can take another step, and then another—until you've stepped right out of your rut. The journey is not always easy and there are no quick fixes, but it does help to have a plan. That's exactly what I hope you'll find in the coming chapters—some simple tried-and-true strategies that can keep you moving in the right direction.

If you keep taking steps, you may eventually remove *worn out* from the list of adjectives that describes you. Instead, there will be words like *alive, caring, confident, purposeful, joyful, vibrant,* and *vital.*

Just the way God planned for you to live.

Something to Try

You can choose just one...

* In your own words, write out the worn-out symptoms you are experiencing. Which one are you most concerned about?

* Identify the people and circumstances that you believe may be contributing to your weariness. What about your own habits and tendencies?

* Take a few minutes to look at the contents page. If you are drawn to some chapters more than others, put a little check by them. Decide whether you are going to read this book straight through or if you prefer to read the chapters you checked first.

* Find an hour or two in the next few days and do something just for yourself. A leisurely walk, a nap in the backyard, curling up with a favorite book, an unhurried lunch with a friend...whatever speaks comfort and relaxation to you.

2

Telling Your Story

ou have a story about what has brought you to this point—a unique story that has been shaped by who you are and what you've done. The people and events in your life have also touched you. Your story probably has dark chapters and happy ones; you may be pleased with certain parts and dissatisfied with others. And sometimes you might wonder if you are too weary to finish well.

Wherever you are in your story, God is your coauthor, and He loves a wonderful ending. But looking back at some early chapters can help you get a sense of what has happened so far and how it might affect you in days to come. More important, it can keep you from slipping back into old, negative patterns.

We aren't saying you have to unravel the past before you start changing the future. You don't. You might even decide to save this "looking back" chapter for later and move ahead with more active solutions. That's okay as long as you eventually give some time to considering what got you into your worn-out ruts in the first place.

So...what's your story? I (Alice) asked several worn-out women to share theirs with me. Although they give only brief glimpses, each story offers some reasons for the present weariness of these women:

Susan describes her early childhood as happy and says that some of her best memories were times spent with her dad. But then, when Susan was eleven, her father's business failed, and he turned to alcohol. From that time forward, Susan's home life was best described as living on a keg of dynamite. Susan never knew what would set her father off, so she dedicated her life to trying to prevent his outbursts by being "perfect." She said she has carried that perfection-ism into her adult life. The trouble is, no matter what she does, she never feels good enough. She can't please every-one. And she is tired of trying.

Beth says she has been quiet and reflective "forever." She can't remember anything traumatic from her child-hood, yet she has always been a worrier, often feeling overwhelmed by the injustices of the world. Now she wor-ries about her children's future and does all she can to make sure they have only the best influences. She is pleased with her home life, but doesn't sleep well because of concerns about "what might happen."

Megan is a dynamo. All the women on her mother's side of the family are superachievers, and Megan herself has received numerous awards. Everyone counts on her and she loves it...or at least she used to. Lately she is beginning to feel frayed at the edges as others lean more and more on her to carry their workload. She is just plain tired from their expectations. Some days she feels like running away from everything.

Ashley is just beginning to escape from the painful and ugly things that happened to her while she was growing up. Her bright personality is starting to blossom, but she still has many days when she wearily struggles with anger and resentment. "On the days when I take intentional steps away from the past," Ashley says, "I notice a light and happy feeling around my heart."

So...what's *your* story? Do you relate to Susan or Beth or Megan or Ashley? As you look at your own life, can you identify elements that might have something to do with feeling worn out? Let's look at just a few of the "story" factors that might hold a clue to the weariness in your life.

Who You Are

God made us all different—that's one of the wonders of His creation. Some people are extroverts, some introverts. Some are scramblers, some amblers. Some are upbeat, some melancholy. Some are directors, some followers. Some are planners, some spontaneous. Some are physically robust, some more delicate.

Your basic personality or temperament is part of the way God wove you in your mother's womb.[1] So is your physical makeup—your height, your build, your nervous system, the fact that you are a woman. Understanding and embracing how you were put together will help you appreciate your story and also give you some clues as to what wears you out.

A bubbly, extroverted woman, for instance, reacts to life differently than someone who is more quiet and reflective. A woman with a tendency toward migraines learns to respond differently to stress than a woman who seldom has a headache. Though none of us is immune from becoming worn out, each of us may become overwhelmed for different reasons and in different ways.

As you consider the ways in which your basic makeup may be contributing to your worn-out tendencies, keep reminding yourself that <u>God did not create you to be exhausted</u>! Although you cannot easily change your basic personality or body type, you can learn to guide and nurture it so it can be a blessing. Ask the Lord to help you use the positive aspects of who you are to bring balance into your life.

32

We don't have ordinary lives.
Not any of us.
Most are extraordinary, and each of us
has had exciting, rich experiences
and a story to tell.

KENNETH HONEYCUTT

The People in Your Life

A friend of mine (Alice) gave me a lovely piece of calligraphy art with a quote about people who "leave their footprints" on our hearts. It hangs above my desk as a reminder of all the people who have influenced my life—role models and mentors, friends and family, those who have taught and encouraged me, and even those who have hurt or hindered me. All these people are an integral part of my story—just as the people in your life are part of yours. As you look into your past for clues to why you feel so worn out, it's a good idea to look at the important people in your life.

Your parents, of course, are a crucial influence—whether they are living or dead and whether they were present or absent in your life when you were growing up. Others in your family of origin—such as grandparents or siblings—may be almost as important. They taught you how to respond to life, and these lessons could contribute to your current levels of weariness.

You may have grown up, for example, with a parent who was sometimes loving and nurturing, but other times was unduly harsh or cruel. Not knowing what to expect, you tried harder and harder to please. Maybe you felt loved by your parents only when you made good grades or excelled in sports. You still feel the pressure. Or perhaps when you were growing up, you were made to feel selfish if you didn't respond to every favor asked, and the guilt followed you into womanhood. *No* may be a hard word for you to say.

But the impact of people in your life is not limited to your earliest influences. Teachers and classmates and coaches, boyfriends and girlfriends, bosses and colleagues and neighbors—any of these may have made a major positive or negative contribution to your life. If you are married or have been married, your spouse is certainly a major influence. So are your children or anyone who shares your home.

As you tell your story to yourself, consider how interactions with people who matter may be influencing your level of weariness. Do admonitions from a feared coach still echo in your head? Does chronic conflict with a wayward child or a passive-aggressive boss drag you down? Are you involved in a toxic friendship that saps your confidence and energy? If so, resolving these relationship problems may give you a surprising energy boost. But try to keep your focus on understanding, not blaming.

Though other people leave footprints on our lives, they don't have the ultimate power to direct our steps. No matter who has influenced your past, with God's help you have the ability to reshape your future through your own choices and through people and influences you choose to have in your life now.

Here's an example. If you did not grow up in a home where you were loved and nurtured in positive ways, you might need to look outside your family for sources of support and guidance. One way to do this is to find a mentor—an older woman who will agree to meet with you several times a month for advice and support. Titus 2 teaches that this is one of the callings God gives to older women. Your pastor or a leader in the women's ministry program may be able to recommend a mentor—or you could simply ask an older woman you admire to meet with you.

It's even possible to find important mentors in the pages of books. As a new Christian, one of my (Alice) favorites was Edith Schaeffer's *The Hidden Art of Homemaking,*[2] which tells of the many opportunities for creative expression that can be found in everyday life. I was especially struck by her account of what she did as a young bride when homeless men came to her house asking for food. She invited the men to wait on the porch while she prepared something for them. The beautiful part of the story is that she did not just give them food. She arranged the hot soup and cookies attractively on a tray, always adding a garnish or some other small decoration to show the vagrants they were valuable. Edith wanted to make sure that even this humble act of feeding the homeless was done as "unto the Lord." This poignant story modeled for me not only how to be compassionate, but also how to do it with simplicity.

What Has Happened?

Some women seem to glide through life like a duck on smooth water, but the truth is that most of us are paddling like crazy trying to keep events from pulling us under. Events—the things that have happened to you in your life—are the third big factor in your story as you learn to rise above your level of weariness.

Psychologists have discovered that traumatic events in the first ten years of childhood have a profound impact on how we handle life. The divorce or death of a parent, any form of abuse, exposure to violence, or extreme poverty can leave lasting scars. Even common experiences such as moving away from a childhood home or being teased in school can affect us. As we grow older, events continue to shape our lives. Everything you have experienced has contributed in some way to who you are today—including the results of your own choices.

As you look back to tell your story, consider what circumstances stand out in your memory. Be especially alert for events, positive or negative, that changed the way you responded to the world. Did a series of achievements boost your self-confidence? Did the death of a child undermine your sense that all is well in the world and make you especially vigilant about hygiene and safety? Any of these past events might hold a clue as to why you are feeling worn down and weary.

If you have had a hard beginning or have many chapters of tears in your story, we won't offend you with trite phrases of comfort. We certainly don't want to trivialize your trauma by claiming "it's God's will" or "it was all for the best." But we do believe that God loves you too much to waste the pain you have experienced. Somehow He can use the hurtful years and in His time weave them into a beautiful part of your story. So we urge you to keep turning toward God in the midst of your painful events instead of away from Him. You *need* God, especially when your life threatens to wear you down.

Do I Need to See a Counselor?

Most worn-out women don't. But consider talking to your family doctor or seeing a counselor if any of the following apply to you:

- You've gone a week or more with very little or no sleep in spite of your attempts to get a good night's rest.
- You've experienced a ten-pound weight gain or loss without your conscious effort and for no discernible medical reason.
- You've had thoughts that life is not worth it anymore.
- You experience consistent feelings that there is nothing positive and there probably never will be.
- You've spent two weeks or more wanting to isolate yourself and doing whatever you can to avoid other people.
- You feel unable to think straight or manage your thoughts.
- You have been sabotaging yourself through your words and actions.
- Your friends and family express concern about your behavior, choices, or emotions.
- You experience a persistent, overwhelming fear that something terrible is going to happen to you or those you love.
- You have noted a long-term pattern of emotional numbness, general dissatisfaction, and/or hard-heartedness.

Your Story and God's Love

As you explore who you are, the people you have known, and what has happened to you, you'll probably begin to get a sense for why you've reached your current weary state. The cause may be outside influences or internal conflicts—most likely it's a combination. Whatever you discover, please keep in mind a few things.

First, telling your story is a tool, not a full-time occupation. It's not really necessary to explore every question and nail down every tendency. Life is a mystery, after all, and you'll never completely sort out all your influences and motivations. But you can still benefit by looking for major events, patterns, choices, and messages that might affect your behavior today.

Remember, too, that it's hard to be objective about your own history. Memory can be faulty, judgment can be clouded, and your emotions can keep you from seeing your past clearly. As you tell your story, pray to God for clarity and then perhaps look for other sources of perspective as well. Writing down what you remember or telling it to a trusted friend can help. So can comparing your memories with someone who shared the experience with you. If the process of telling your story becomes difficult or stirs up very painful emotions, consider the questions on the previous page to determine if you should seek the help of a professional counselor.

The most important thing to remember as you tell your story to yourself is that it's not finished! God is working as your very creative coauthor, and His influence is always loving.

One of my favorite word pictures from the Bible is from Song of Solomon: "His banner over me is love."[3] The Lord's banner over your story is not disdain or judgment, but love. He knew the end of your story before it ever began, and through it all He covers you with compassion. No matter what chapters are in your past or what chapters are yet to be written, you are tenderly and completely loved.

Remember when you were a young girl and wondered if some boy loved you? Like a detective searching for proof, you picked a daisy and began pulling the delicate white petals. *He loves me...he loves me not. He loves me...he loves me not.* Wondering how the daisy game would end.

It is so different with the Lord. You never have to wonder. He loves you.

He loves you.

He loves you.

He loves you.

No matter what your story, He will *always* love you.

Something to Try

You can choose just one...

✳ Describe the parts of your personality that you consider to be the most positive. Find a quiet place where you can get on your knees, and thank God for that part of who you are.

✳ Write down your unique story, including the key people and events that helped shape you into the person you are today. Describe when and why you started to feel worn out.

✳ Find the following verses in the Bible, and read them aloud: Zephaniah 3:17; Romans 8:38–39; Ephesians 3:14–19. Put a heart by your favorite phrases. Then take a lipstick and write "Jesus loves me! This I know, for the Bible tells me so" on your bathroom mirror.

✳ Tonight, if the weather is clear, step outside and spend some time stargazing. If it is stormy, linger a while just outside your door. Let the wind mess up your hair, and drink in the fragrance of the rain. No matter what your story, revel in the present gift of being alive.

3

*Should*s and *Ought*s

> I cannot give you the formula for success,
> but I can give you the formula for failure...
> which is: Try to please everyone.

HERBERT BAYARD SWOPE

t was a nightmare—or at least a very bad dream.

Rebecca was preparing to go to the most important meeting of her life. In fact, she was the keynote speaker. If she was liked and accepted by those present, wonderful things would happen. If she wasn't, she felt like the rest of her life would be plagued by misery. The people at this meeting were very particular about how things should be done, and they were easily offended if anything went inappropriately. They had sent Rebecca detailed instructions on what to wear, what to say, and how to act—but she had lost the instructions.

Time was ticking away and Rebecca had only an hour before she had to leave. But she didn't know what to wear, let alone what to do. She stood paralyzed before her closet as feelings of panic overwhelmed her.

Rebecca woke with her heart racing. Her eyes darted around the darkened room as she gradually realized it had all been a dream.

Dreams are often pictures of our emotions, and this was true for Rebecca. She did have an important speaking event coming up. And although there were no lost instructions, she felt the pressure of expectations—a pressure that had spilled over into her dreams.

Most worn-out women struggle with expectations. Do you ever feel like an octopus is attacking you, its arms grabbing and pulling? Everyone seems to want more and more. They want you to do things better and bigger and quicker, all the while with a smile on your face. Everywhere you turn, there's another expectation...until you're exhausted just thinking about it. Your family, your friends, your work, your neighbors, and even your church have expectations for you. You have expectations for yourself as well.

It's too much. Yet the *should*s and *ought*s don't stop. As they grow, you can feel the arms of the octopus wrapping tighter.

What can you do? The only way to stop the octopus from dragging you down is to starve it. If you take away the three foods it thrives on, the octopus will lose its power, and overwhelming expectations will lose their grip. The three foods are comparison, people pleasing, and perfectionism. Let's look at each one.

Comparison

Comparing yourself to others is dangerous, especially when you are on the verge of being worn out. As your stress increases, you tend to become more self-critical. Whoever you are, someone will always be better or brighter than you, and comparisons can cause envy, competitiveness, and dissatisfaction.

When you compare yourself to others, you actually stop seeing yourself. All you see is how you measure up to your perception of someone else. Comparisons accomplish nothing except to increase expectations. This saps your energy and kills your morale. It is one more standard to live up to and one more burden to bear.

The most common areas in which people compare themselves can be thought of as the "six *A*s":

* **A**ppearance—how we look. "I would do anything to have thighs that slim."

* **A**rticulation—how we speak. "She's always quick with an answer while I'm just fumbling for words."

* **A**ttitude—how we think. "It's easy for her to be upbeat; she's just naturally good natured."

* **A**ccomplishments—what we do. "Yeah, I could finish my degree too if I didn't have to work full-time."

* **A**cquisition—what we have. "Well, it's obvious she never has to shop at Bargain Mart. Some people have all the luck."

* **A**bility—where we excel. "Even if I practiced, I could never play the piano like she does. She's just a natural."

In these areas of comparison, most of us tend to exaggerate the other person's qualities while minimizing our ally we might try to bolster our self-confidence ne quality, hoping no one will notice our per- ncies. Either way, we put unnecessary stress on ourselves.

How can we fight this natural tendency to compare ourselves with others? The best antidote is a healthy dose of reality. The apostle Paul puts it this way: "Try to have a sane estimate of your capabilities."[1] Each person is unique, with a specific God-given set of attributes and abilities. Each of us has areas where we can grow and improve, but in God's eyes, comparisons between people are like comparisons between roses and lilies—both are beautiful.

In any given area, someone will always be better or worse than we are. In an overall comparison, we are simply individual and therefore incomparable. More important, we are each infinitely precious to our heavenly Father. He sees us as we are and still loves us.[2] When we truly take this to heart, we will have far less need to compare ourselves with others.

To get a better sense of this, you might try looking at the list of "100 Positives" found on the next page. Highlight or circle the ones that apply to you. Ask a trusted friend to look at the list to see if there are any positives you missed. Spend some time thinking about your positive characteristics. Then resolve to start accepting yourself, respecting yourself, loving yourself, and thanking God for how He made you. We all need to spend less time looking around and more time looking up.

The 100 Positives

1. Accepting 2. Agreeable 3. Ambitious 4. Appreciative
5. Attentive 6. Available 7. Brave 8. Calm 9. Caring
10. Cheerful 11. Clean 12. Clever 13. Committed
14. Compassionate 15. Concerned 16. Conscientious
17. Consistent 18. Considerate 19. Content 20. Cooperative
21. Courteous 22. Curious 23. Dependable 24. Determined
25. Diligent 26. Discerning 27. Disciplined 28. Encouraging
29. Enthusiastic 30. Fair 31. Faithful 32. Flexible
33. Forgiving 34. Friendly 35. Generous 36. Gentle
37. Giving 38. Godly 39. Graceful 40. Grateful 41. Happy
42. Helpful 43. Honest 44. Hospitable 45. Humble
46. Industrious 47. Ingenious 48. Insightful 49. Joyful
50. Kind 51. Loving 52. Loyal 53. Mature 54. Meek
55. Merciful 56. Modest 57. Moral 58. Neat 59. Observant
60. Optimistic 61. Organized 62. Patient 63. Peaceful
64. Persistent 65. Playful 66. Polite 67. Positive 68. Principled
69. Punctual 70. Reassuring 71. Relaxed 72. Reliable
73. Reflective 74. Respectful 75. Responsible 76. Reverent
77. Satisfied 78. Secure 79. Self-controlled 80. Sensible
81. Sensitive 82. Sincere 83. Sociable 84. Steadfast
85. Straightforward 86. Supportive 87. Sympathetic
88. Tactful 89. Teachable 90. Tender 91. Thorough
92. Thoughtful 93. Trustworthy 94. Truthful
95. Understanding 96. Unselfish 97. Virtuous 98. Well-mannered 99. Willing 100. Wise

People Pleasing

"My life was about three things: pleasing, proving, and achieving," remembers author and speaker Mary Lyn Miller about a time in her life when she was a "people pleaser." "I thought that if enough people liked me, I would feel better about being me. I wanted desperately to please everyone...family, bosses, neighbors, people I didn't like."[3]

Does this sound like you? Many people, especially women, have a bad case of what has been popularly called the "disease to please"—and it's an energy-sapping malady. If you're not sure whether you're a people pleaser, ask yourself these questions:

- ✳ Do I work overtime to impress those around me?
- ✳ Do I often say yes when I really want to say no?
- ✳ Do I depend too much on compliments and affirmations to feel good?
- ✳ Do I let others schedule my priorities or activities?
- ✳ Do I try too hard to be nice?
- ✳ Do I take criticism too personally?
- ✳ Do I find it hard to be firm?
- ✳ Do I feel very bad when someone is upset at me?
- ✳ Do I apologize when I don't need to?
- ✳ Do I bend over backward for other people, even when part of me is protesting and resentful?

Don't misunderstand. Nothing is inherently wrong with being nice or accommodating, unless it's for the wrong reasons. If you're accommodating others because you fear they won't like you or will reject you, that's the wrong reason. People pleasing essentially means letting other people's imagined expectations control your answers. Trying to do that on a consistent basis will simply wear you out.

Constantly trying to please others is not only draining; it is also an impossible task. What makes some people happy makes others angry. What makes some applaud alienates others. You might try to please, only to find you have offended. Seeking to please is like trying to catch a snowflake on your tongue; even if you can do it, it doesn't last very long.

There is another problem with people pleasing. If you take extraordinary measures and *succeed* in pleasing them, they'll expect extraordinary measures and more the next time. When you work harder and longer, they again raise their standards. Trying to please and to meet the expectations of others can quickly become a vicious cycle.

It's natural to want people to like you. It's natural to want them to respect and think well of you. But if this desire drives you to be a worn-out woman, it's time to stop. Remember that your physical, emotional, and spiritual health is more important than temporarily pleasing someone else.

Scripture reminds us that "our purpose is to please God, not people."[4] I (Steve) like the way my friend Allison put it: "I realize that everybody has a plan for my life and talents, but my only pursuit needs to be that which God has planned for me. Some people won't like it, but I don't lose any sleep over it."

If you can get to the point where you can say that honestly, you'll cut your stress dramatically. Pleasing people can lead you astray, but pleasing God *never* will.

Perfectionism

Perfection doesn't exist on this planet, but that doesn't stop a lot of us from trying to achieve it! Many women secretly believe they must be perfect, or nearly perfect, in everything they do. They may give lip service to "nobody's perfect," but the despair they feel when they fail reveals their perfectionism.

Perfectionists strive for the unattainable. They need to be first or best and try never to make a mistake, which they see as a sign of failure and unworthiness. Because of this, perfectionists are rarely happy. They frequently slip into depression and are often disappointed. Sometimes they're so worn out by their own expectations that they fail to do anything at all.

Use what talents you possess:
The woods would be very silent
If no birds sang
Except those that sang best.

HENRY VAN DYKE

At the heart of perfectionism is fear—fear of making a mistake and being judged, fear of failure and rejection. The faulty belief underlying perfectionist behavior is this: *If I could get everything right, life would be good. People would love me, and then I could finally love myself.* The problem is that as soon as you think you have everything right, something goes wrong.

At an even deeper level, perfectionism reveals a lack of faith. In a sense, perfectionism is really a way of playing God with our own lives. Instead of trusting God to keep His promise to redeem us and mature us, instead of walking in obedience, we try to preempt His work and get it right without His help. No wonder we're exhausted!

It's true that some translations of certain verses of the Bible (such as James 1:4) exhort us to "be perfect." But if you read these verses in context, you'll see that "perfect" is used in the sense of being complete or mature, not never making mistakes. And these verses also make it clear that achieving this kind of "perfection" is a gradual process achieved by the Holy Spirit working in us. It's not something we're supposed to achieve on our own, and trying will only wear us out.

With all that in mind, here are a few principles to help you fight perfectionism:

Admit that perfection is impossible. No one you know is perfect, and nothing you do will be perfect. That's just reality. The harder you try to reach the unattainable, the more frustrated, exhausted, and defeated you will feel.

🌼 *Give yourself permission to make mistakes.* Do it out loud—actually tell yourself in the mirror, "Mistakes are all right." In his book *Perfection,* Dr. David Burns says, "If people can't accept your imperfections, that's their fault." Expectations of a mistake-free life are heavier burdens than God would ever place on us.

🌼 *Accept your weaknesses and failures.* They are an inescapable part of being human. Have the humility to stop pretending you have it all together. You blow it every day, and this very failure can help you learn and grow.

🌼 *Set realistic and reachable goals.* Nothing is more discouraging than attempting to do what can't be done. Do what is doable and give yourself credit for each day's accomplishments.

🌼 *Aim for excellence, not perfection.* Completing a task well is important, but don't confuse excellence with perfection. You can achieve excellence in some areas, but perfection belongs to God.

Giving up perfectionism isn't easy. Sometimes the distinction between unhealthy perfectionism and healthy high standards is hard to see. But the advantages of "living human" are so strong that overcoming perfectionism is worth the effort.

As you begin letting go of your drive for perfection, you might be amazed at the results. As you accept your own humanity and begin to lean on God, you will start to relax and enjoy life. Your relationships will improve as you erase your perfectionism standards for others. And interestingly enough, as you accept your failings and learn from them, you may find yourself achieving far more than you ever could before.

Living with Expectations

Life will always be full of expectations, your own and others'. How you respond to them will determine how worn out you become. The key, of course, is to stop letting others control you through their expectations. Instead, you can listen to God, trust Him, obey Him, be guided by His expectations. He is the one who knows all things, understands all things, and can help you through all things—the only one who can keep the octopus of expectations off your back.

What a God!

What a relief!

Something to Try

You can choose just one...

* Look again at the qualities you circled on the list of "100 Positives" (p. 45). On a three-by-five card, write your favorites and keep them someplace where you can refer to them often.

* Discuss the following idea with a friend: "You don't have to be perfect to be wonderful."

* Write down some of the expectations—your own or others'—that tend to drive your life. Identify any that seem difficult or unreasonable, and create some boundaries to help you stand up to those expectations. If your outside work tends to encroach on your home life, for instance, try resolving: "I will not work after five in the evening or on the weekends." If necessary, discuss your new boundaries with the people they affect.

* Try planting an indoor garden in a sunny window of your kitchen or dining area. A favorite is a lemon herb garden because it gives a tart fragrance to the room.

Time for a Change

Time is a dressmaker specializing in alterations.

FAITH BALDWIN

geri was experiencing the start of a typical day. Up before the rest of the family, she planned to spend a little time reading her new devotional book and praying. Before finishing the first paragraph, however, she remembered her teenage son's basketball uniform was still in the washing machine. She'd thrown it in the washer late last night but had fallen asleep on the couch before the wash cycle ended. She decided to stop reading for just a minute to run and pop the uniform in the dryer so it would be ready before Brian left for school.

She hoped Brian had remembered to gas up his car yesterday. He'd been late to school twice this week, and one more tardy would mean he couldn't start in the game that night. Maybe she'd better check to see if his alarm was set early enough to allow time to get gas.

On the way to her son's room, Geri's mind raced ahead to her nine-thirty meeting. Why was she dreading it? She knew everyone would love her ideas. She had a reputation for success, even if it did mean topping herself each time. Maybe she dreaded the meeting because she knew the rest of the team would applaud the plan, but most of the responsibility for carrying it out would fall on her. That was the worst part of being a great idea person.

Geri had planned to make homemade cinnamon rolls to take to the meeting, but she'd been too exhausted last night, and there wasn't time this morning. She could call Judy and ask her to pick up some doughnuts, but Geri always hated to inconvenience anyone on such short notice. Oh well, she could leave a few minutes early and pick up the doughnuts herself. *If only I had two more hours each day, then I could get everything finished. The new devotional book can wait until tomorrow, and surely God understands if I have to say my prayers on the run.*

Geri's day, like the days of many worn-out women, is full of things she really doesn't want to do or things she really shouldn't do—but she is likely to keep doing them anyway. The praise and admiration she gets from her family and friends (yes, she is a people pleaser!) give her a temporary feeling of satisfaction, so she tries to ignore the fatigue that starts in the morning and hangs around all day. But no matter how many things she accomplishes, a sense of purpose and fulfillment eludes her because Geri is missing the call God has on her life. She has no space left in her day even for listening to Him, much less for following where He might lead.

It's so easy for women to fall into a pattern of reacting to the demands of others instead of actively choosing how they want to invest their lives. And even when they sense that they're wasting precious time and energy, sometimes they just don't know how to stop.

I (Alice) know. I've been there. But I've also discovered four important principles that have helped me open up some time for exploring God's plan for me. Try them. You'll be surprised how your world brightens when you make even small changes to free up time for really listening to what the Lord has to say.

Time-Clearing Principle #1:
"You Can Do It All" Really Is a Myth

Let's be honest. Most of us overcrowd our schedules because we want to. That's true for Geri, and it's also true for us. We say yes to projects that interest us, to commitments that offer temporary satisfaction or the approval of others, and to jobs we think we should do. Most of the items on our to-do lists are good and worthwhile—at least on the surface. And though we give lip service to the notion that we can't do it all, we'd still like to try.

The problem is that we really *can't* do it all—and if we try, the items we never get to are sometimes the most important ones. Overcommitment is not only exhausting; it also makes maintaining balance almost impossible because "urgent" issues will almost always crowd out those that are more important but less time sensitive. We quickly reach the point where we are routinely postponing time with the Lord and with family and friends in favor of "getting things done"—even replacing meaningful relationships with the temporary rewards of trying to live up to everyone's expectations.

Over the years I have often fallen into that rabbit hole. And like another Alice (the one who visited Wonderland), I found it difficult—though not impossible—to get out once I'd fallen in.

Something as simple as changing the style of my appointment calendar has helped me. This year I bought a slim pocket calendar without spaces to schedule every half hour. The section for "must do" items is small, leaving more space in my day for "want to dos."

Here's another idea that has helped: Whenever I wonder if I'm making a difference in my world, I resist the temptation to answer that question with my to-do list. Instead, I look around at my family and friends and see how I'm responding to them. If my relationships are strong, I decide I'm doing all right. It's a good feeling.

Have you ever wondered what Jesus' appointment book would have looked like if He'd kept one? Someone once suggested that written across every page would be just a few words: "To do the will of my Father." I'm not sure I'm quite ready to change my calendar that much, but I find that keeping that picture in mind really helps me reserve space for unscheduled listening and following.

Time-Clearing Principle #2:
Helping Is Not Always Helping

Geri is a good mom and desperately wants her children to succeed. Unfortunately, that means she is doing things for her teenage son—like doing his laundry and making sure he gets to school on time—that he is perfectly capable of doing himself. She is afraid he won't manage, so she hovers over him, hoping to protect him from making mistakes. What she's really doing is gratifying her need for control and trying to protect her image of being a good parent. In the process, she's depriving her son of the valuable opportunity to learn responsibility...and she's also wearing herself out.

If you let it, the desire for control and protection will flow into all areas of your life. You'll take on the leadership of a committee or a project just so you can make sure everything is done the way you think is best. You'll find it hard to delegate because you feed yourself the overused line, "It's easier to do it myself." And maybe that's true—but only in the short term.

Delegating tasks and responsibility is a wonderful way to mentor others. Teaching and encouraging may indeed take extra effort on your part, but only at the beginning. Before you know it, your children or junior coworkers will be flying on their own, developing valuable skills—and helping you! Allowing people to learn through their own mistakes and successes is a gift you give to others. At the same time, you will be giving yourself the precious gift of time.

57

Time-Clearing Principle #3:
Practice Responsible Procrastination

Isn't this a wonderful phrase? At first it seems like a paradox, but with a second reading you realize it's not a contradiction at all. You get a sense of empowerment when you choose *not* to do everything on your urgent list.

This is a concept that has never occurred to Geri. She thinks that everything needs to be done *now*. Except, that is, the things that matter most in the long run.

The darn trouble with cleaning the house is it gets dirty the next day anyway. So skip a week if you have to.

BARBARA BUSH

58

I remember a day when I had planned to organize my closets. Right before I started, the phone rang. My friend Barbara said, "I'm missing you, and I wish you were here with me with our feet propped up on the coffee table while we drink coffee and eat chocolate." I hung up the phone and drove right over to her house. It was a good choice. I forgot all about my neatnik closets, and *no one cared.*

I realize that many of you yearn for the chance to drop everything and visit a friend, but you can't because you are in a different season of life than I am. You may be caring for young children and working full time, and you simply can't let those major tasks slide. Even so, I urge you to try to find some items on your to-do list where you can responsibly procrastinate. Instead of spending all your time on *ought*s and *should*s, try to steal a little time for a favorite activity.

Remember, we're not recommending procrastination as a general policy. It goes without saying that such a habit can lead to serious problems—that's why we included the word *responsible*. When you procrastinate responsibly, you're not just blowing off all your commitments; you're taking some time to carefully consider those commitments and decide if they are truly urgent. If they aren't, you have the freedom to delay projects or even not to do them at all.

I have found that delaying a little bit often helps me see that the item I thought I *had* to do isn't really so important. Sometimes I find myself crossing it off my list altogether. And I've found that crossing off a to-do item because it's not that important feels really good.

And here's a truly liberating thought: The fact that you have a good idea doesn't mean you have to carry it through to completion—and you certainly don't have to do it right away. Maybe you can pass along the idea to others. Maybe you can put it on a "someday" list, or perhaps it will always remain a delicious possibility. If you let yourself procrastinate a little—responsibly—you'll probably know just what to do when the time comes.

Time-Clearing Principle #4:
Delay Saying Yes...and Learn to Say No

When Geri starts sharing her great ideas at the meeting, she'll be asked to head up another project. Riding high on enthusiasm and addicted to success, she will probably say yes and then regret it later.

Most of us are tempted to respond immediately to requests. We're almost programmed that way—and our first instinct is to say yes. We're flattered to be asked. We like the feeling of being needed. And we're willing to overlook the important difference between being asked and being called.

I've found I can short-circuit this process if I can delay my yes long enough to seriously seek God's direction. Along with praying and looking for answers in the Bible, we need to ask ourselves some hard questions.

- How does this fit in with my other priorities?
- Do I have the time, energy, and resources to carry through with this project?
- How will this commitment affect those I love?
- What do my friends and family think about my taking on another commitment?
- Can someone else do the job better than I could?

If your schedule is already full, a simple rule is to never add any new responsibility until you have eliminated something else. If you can't do that, then the appropriate answer is probably no.

Is *no* a hard word for you to say? It is for many women. But if you want to clear more time for following what God wants you to do, you simply have to get comfortable with the word *no*. You must learn *when* to say it and possibly how to say it as well.

Years ago I found some tips in a magazine on how to say no. I've included them in the sidebar below. I don't have the original author's name, but I love what she wrote. The words are humorous at times, but they actually work. I encourage you to practice daily so they're on the tip of your tongue whenever you need them—which may be more often than you think. If you want to be available to say yes to God's call on your life, you're going to have to say no to something else.

How to Say No

To learn to say no, put your tongue on the roof of your mouth and say ...

- ✴ I'll have to pass it up.
- ✴ I've done it in the past. I'll do it again in the future. But I can't do it right now.
- ✴ I'm sorry, but my schedule doesn't permit me to take on any more obligations this week, this month, this year, this decade!
- ✴ It was very kind of you to ask me, but I really must say no.

🌼 I've made a mistake. I shouldn't have committed
myself. I'm sorry, but I really must back out this time.

🌼 *For special occasions:* I cannot do this. I don't have
the desire, the time, the interest, or the energy. NO.
Absolutely not!

AUTHOR UNKNOWN

Beside Still Waters

At the beginning of this chapter, we only peeked at Geri's
morning. But the rest of her week looks the same.
Morning until night she multitasks, jamming everything
she can into her schedule, and still doesn't finish. Her
wish for just two more hours a day is a revealing signal
that she has taken on more than God ever desired for her
to do.

There is a longing in my heart to come alongside all the
Geris in this world. If we could walk together for a while, I
would share my regrets about pushing the limits for too
many years. Friend to friend, we could talk about the value
of listening to God and taking care of ourselves, of reserv-
ing more empty places on our calendars, of treasuring
relationships more than accomplishments.

Our journey would take us along a quiet path and over
a little stone bridge to an open meadow. Kicking off our
shoes and lying back in the grass, our faces turned to the
warm sun, we would softly recite together Psalm 23. As our
duet reached the words,

He makes me lie down in green pastures,
he leads me beside quiet waters,
he restores my soul,[1]

we would smile, knowing this is God's pleasure.

Just a typical day—full and purposeful, but with time to spare for eternity.

Something to Try

You can choose just one...

- Make a list of some fun or relaxing things you want to do. Each week find one thing on your priority list, and try responsible procrastination. Put it off for at least three days and do something fun instead.

- Choose at least one responsibility you take care of consistently and delegate it to someone else.

- Look for a time this week when you can practice using one of the "How to Say No" tips. Don't worry about how people will react; if you know you should say no, then take a deep breath and say it.

- One of the most often quoted portions of Psalm 23 is "He leads me beside quiet waters, he restores my soul" (NIV). Remember a place you've been that epitomizes "still waters" in your mind. (It doesn't have to have water; it's the sense of peace you're looking for.) Close your eyes, kick off your shoes, and imagine you are there.

5

Playing to Your Strengths

It's never too late to be what you might have been.

Mary Ann Evans

elody hated her job. She dreaded each day she had to go to work.

Melody was an extrovert, with a gift for motivating and relating to others. She loved people, and everybody loved her, but her job involved sitting alone in a small office managing files and balancing ledgers. She had never much liked organizational or mathematical tasks, but that is what her job required.

Being a responsible person, Melody worked hard and did a competent job, but there was no joy in what she did. Over time, the demands of her job drained the joy out of every aspect of her life—her marriage, her parenting, her friendships, her hobbies, her faith. By thirty-five she was so worn out she had even considered abandoning her family and moving to some tropical location to work at a vacation resort.

"What is so attractive about your fantasy?" I (Steve) asked Melody when she came to me for counseling.

"Quitting my job and getting to work with people."

"Well," I responded, "Why can't you do that now?"

With some encouragement, Melody found a new job in public relations where she can use her motivational and social strengths. Today she is a new person—exciting, exuberant, fun loving. She is full of smiles, which she shares with everybody she meets. And though she still works hard, she seems to have energy to spare.

"How worn out do you feel?" I asked her recently.

Melody burst into a contagious laugh. "Worn out? I don't even remember the word."

Too often the worn-out woman is working hard at what she is asked to do and is doing a good job, but simply is not enjoying herself.

Is that true for you? Is your daily work—whether at an office, in your home, or where you volunteer—just a set of tasks you grind out because you need to? You may be gratified by the praise of others or find a generic satisfaction in just getting the job done. But wouldn't it feel wonderful to love what you're doing—really love it? To be excited and energized and empowered by each task? That's what it feels like to live inside your strengths.

For many women this idea raises its own set of frustrations. Some aren't sure they *have* any strengths or gifts. (*I'm just not that good at anything.*) Others can't believe they can reconcile their talents and desires with the life they've chosen. (*I'd like to do something else, but I can't let everyone down.*) Some are good at what they do but feel drawn to something they've never tried. (*I love being a full-time mother, but I still dream of being a travel agent someday.*)

In an ideal world, we'd all spend our working hours—whether at home or away—on pursuits that suit our talents and interests and reflect God's calling. In this fallen world, it's not always that easy. But it's almost always possible to adjust our lives to fit our God-given strengths more closely—and rediscover the joy and zest God intends for our lives.

The longings of your heart are not incidental;
they are critical messages.
The desires of your heart are not to be ignored,
they are to be consulted.
As the wind turns the weather vane,
so God used your passions to turn your life.

MAX LUCADO[1]

What's My Gift?

I (Steve) have always enjoyed those puzzles that are full of hidden objects, but every once in a while something blends in so well that it might as well be invisible. One day I was trying to find a horse in just such a picture. I looked and looked, but I couldn't see it. It didn't help that a friend was watching over my shoulder, telling me the horse was so obvious that if it were real it would bite me.

Finally, in frustration, I gave up. "Go ahead and show me where this stupid horse is hiding."

She pointed, and I couldn't believe I'd missed it! The problem was that I had focused on the wrong elements of the picture. Once I knew where to look, I saw the horse as clearly as if it were never hidden.

Your strengths can be like this. If you're not sure where to focus, it might seem like they don't exist. Or maybe you know you have several strengths and talents, but you aren't sure which to develop. Finding your best abilities starts with answering a few easy questions.

- What were your favorite subjects in school?
- What do you enjoy doing in your free time?
- In what areas do you get the most compliments?
- What do you feel most comfortable and confident doing?
- What things do your friends think you're best at?
- What pursuits seem to come most naturally to you?
- What do you have fun doing? (It's okay to consider this. Really!)
- What activities keep calling to you strongly, even if you're not sure you'd be good at them?

I believe this last question is especially important. Your areas of strength often are those in which you're most talented or you're "good at." Or perhaps there are areas where you have (or think you have) limited talent or ability but have intense interest or passion. Or they may be areas to which God is calling you specifically and for which He will equip you.

You will probably find your greatest strengths at the point where your natural talents, passions, and sense of God's calling intersect. The more hours you spend using that strength, the less stressed you are likely to feel.

What Are My Options?

The brilliant composer Ludwig van Beethoven had difficulty solving the most elementary arithmetic problem. C. S. Lewis, Oxford professor and literary genius, was so nonmechanical that he couldn't figure out how to use a simple typewriter or almost any other mechanical device.[2]

Chances are, you too are great in some areas, competent in others, and a bit challenged (or very challenged) in others. It probably makes sense, then, to choose your greatest strengths and build on what you have. If you have verbal strengths, you'll want to develop your public speaking or writing skills. If you are artistic, you can look for opportunities to practice and improve those mediums of expression in which God has gifted you. On the other hand, if you struggle with math, you probably don't want to pursue accounting or volunteer to be PTA treasurer. Or if organization seems to elude you, that administrative assistant job is likely not for you, and don't even think about volunteering to chair the church fundraising campaign!

God-given dreams, interests, and passions are all part of the equation. Often they will help you decide between options. You may have artistic talent, for instance, but the solitary, precarious life of a painter just doesn't appeal to you. However you may thrive as an interior decorator or be completely energized helping a group of children paint murals on the walls of the church nursery.

If you're still struggling to get a handle on what your area of strength may be, the following list may help. Look over the twelve statements below, and circle the ones that ring true for you:

❋ You love playing with words and excel in speaking and writing.

❋ You get excited by expressing yourself in artistic areas and may have been told you have artistic talent.

❋ You love to organize and have a knack for bringing order to chaos.

❋ You are a natural encourager and motivator.

❋ You enjoy having people in your home and hostessing special events.

❋ You are energized by numbers and finances.

❋ You find pleasure in expressing yourself musically.

❋ You like to fix and repair things.

❋ You are comfortable in leadership roles or people frequently look to you for direction.

❋ You often find fulfillment behind the scenes, helping and serving.

✳ You relish athletic challenges and hands-on activities.

✳ You are drawn to research and problem solving.

Do one or two of these descriptions seem to fit you? Do any of them catch your interest or call to you? If so, why not take the hint? Pick the one or two that feel most likely, focus on them, and start to dream of the incredible relief of working or volunteering in areas that really energize you.

Use What You've Been Given

Your gifts and abilities are part of God's purpose for your life. Not using them can lead to frustration, disappointment, and fatigue. So when you've pinpointed your strengths, it's important to look for opportunities and environments where you can use them.

Working with your strengths may mean changing jobs, as it did for Melody. It may mean adjusting your responsibilities at your current job or developing a hobby or volunteer position. Almost certainly it will mean you must jettison tasks from your schedule to make room for more appropriate ones. Whatever you do, you will live more joyfully and productively if you take some time to discover your strengths and use them in your life.

It's all right to take small steps, especially at first. If you are feeling worn out, you probably don't have time or energy to do much more. Start by writing down some ideas and possibilities that occur to you. Do a little research and ask advice. Pray for God to point you in the right direction, and watch for the opportunities He brings.

What you are passionate about was created in you to make a splash in this life that no one else can make.

NICOLE JOHNSON[3]

A Word About Spiritual Gifts

While you're trying to understand your strengths, of course, you'll want to consider another important area—your spiritual gifts. The Bible makes it clear that the Holy Spirit equips each member of the body of Christ with specific abilities. In Romans 12, Paul mentions a number of spiritual gifts such as serving, teaching, encouragement, giving, leadership, and mercy.[4] He makes it clear that these gifts are given for the express purpose of building up the community of Christians and that the different spiritual gifts are to complement one another.

How do you determine your spiritual gifts? They will usually, but not always, be congruent with your natural abilities and strengths. A person with verbal talents, for instance, may also find she has the gift of teaching...or she may be surprised to discover a gift for mercy or faith. Finding your specific spiritual gifts and putting them to work for Christ's kingdom is a matter for prayer and discernment, perhaps with the help of a mentor, your pastor, or a spiritual director. Choosing an area of service that uses your spiritual gifts will empower and energize you, for you will be working in the strength of the Spirit.

Living As a Faithful Servant

It's hard to underestimate the importance of finding your fit. When you discover your strengths and learn to work within them, those worn-out feelings will be replaced by a sense of joy and satisfaction that helps you realize what life is supposed to be like. Remember Jesus' words to those who used their talents: "Well done, good and faithful servant!"[5] That's exactly the kind of joy and satisfaction our friend Jane received.

Jane was not brilliant or beautiful or talented. She stuttered slightly and therefore felt uncomfortable in front of more than a couple people. She had a back-breaking job that paid twenty-five cents above minimum wage. Each night she came home exhausted to a small, mostly empty apartment. When she was younger she had been engaged, but two weeks before the wedding her fiancé found someone he liked better.

In a youth-oriented, fashion-conscious, high achievement culture, you'd think Jane wouldn't have a lot to offer. But you'd be terribly wrong!

Jane taught fourth graders in Sunday school for twenty

years, and they loved her. When she walked into a room, every face would brighten as each child tried to get as close to her as possible. Every week her mailbox would hold wedding invitations, birth announcements, and letters of appreciation from past students. Jane responded to each one. On her fiftieth birthday she received nearly a hundred cards.

This woman didn't have a lot of showy abilities, but she made the most of the strengths she had. She had a gift for inspiring and motivating children. She loved them, and they knew it. When Jane passed away last spring, the church couldn't hold all the people who came to her funeral. During the ceremony, hundreds of former students stood with tear-filled eyes and told how Jane had changed their lives.

Jane was about as far from being a worn-out woman as possible because she was wise enough to invest her life in developing her strengths and furthering God's kingdom.

Those who didn't know her well called her "Plain Jane."

Everyone else called her a "good and faithful servant."

Something to Try

You can choose just one...

※ Decide which strengths and gifts on pages 70–71
apply to you. If you have others, add them to the list.
Choose one thing you would love to do in the next
month that will allow you to use that gift.

※ List five things you have accomplished in the past
that gave you great joy and satisfaction. What can
you learn about your strengths from these accomplishments?

※ If you could really find your fit, how would it change
your life? Write an adjective or word picture
describing how you think this would make you feel.

※ Pretend *you* are an important visitor in your home.
Light a fragrant candle, sit in your most comfortable
chair, put on a soothing CD, and breathe deeply.
Don't hurry. Just enjoy these pampering moments.

6

When Your Lamp Burns Low

*Lighthouse people have a way of
leading others out of darkness and
guiding them back to safety.*

JONI EARECKSON TADA

ong ago there was a lighthouse keeper in charge of
keeping the oil light burning so sailors could safely
navigate along a dangerous stretch of the Atlantic
coastline. Once a month he received a supply of oil.
Since the lighthouse was near a coastal village, the
lighthouse keeper had frequent visitors—and most of them
needed to borrow a little oil. One woman needed oil to keep
her family warm. Another guest needed oil for his lamps.
Other visitors also had what seemed to be genuine needs,
and the kind lighthouse keeper tried to meet them all.

Toward the end of one month a terrible storm hit the
rocky coastline. The faithful lighthouse keeper was at his
position tending the lamp so ships could safely pass. But
before dawn, while the storm still raged and the ships were
being tossed by terrifying winds and crashing waves, the oil
ran out and the lighthouse went dark.[1]

Since you have chosen to read this book, I (Alice) think I know some things about you. You are hardworking and generous. You are probably the kind of woman who is willing to give up your piece of dessert if there is not enough to go around. If someone needs a favor, you do it—even if helping means setting aside what you wanted to do. When it comes to making dreams come true, you may lavish your time and money on others while your own precious dreams remain longings.

For as far back as you can remember, your schedule has been too full. Spoonful by spoonful you generously give away your oil. You are truly a wonder, and we love it that you are so tenderhearted and kind. But, dear one, only a little oil is left in your lamp, and we worry that you are burning out before you find the places where God meant your light to shine.

What God Has in Mind for You

Dr. Lloyd John Ogilvie, former chaplain of the United States Senate, tells about when he was still pastor of the First Presbyterian Church in Hollywood, California.

After one service an elderly woman took him by the hand, looked piercingly into his eyes, and said, "I pray your life will be as wonderful as it was in the mind of God when He created you." Immediately Dr. Ogilvie returned to his study, got down on his knees, and pleaded with God to show him exactly what He had in mind.[2]

Scripture tells us, "Don't act thoughtlessly, but try to find out and do whatever the Lord wants you to."[3] His calling is specific and personal. God has a job (or jobs) specially designed for each of us, and He's placed a yearning in our hearts to do just that. Like Dr. Ogilvie, we need to get down on our knees and plead with God to show us what He had in mind when He created us. If we're not honoring His call on our life, we're probably wasting precious energy—and wearing ourselves out.

Making Room for "Someday"

I used to wonder whether finding a specific purpose in life was all that important. What was wrong, I reasoned, with just getting up each morning when the alarm went off and doing whatever good thing came my way? Wasn't that "being available" to God?

The problem for me was that too many things came my way, and I had no time left to pursue what might energize me and really make a difference in the world. My schedule was always full, but there was an empty place in my heart. God-given passions were forgotten on a page of my Day-Timer titled "Someday." My lamp kept burning, but not very brightly.

One day, when I was in one of my fed-up, hurry-up, always catching-up moods, I decided to schedule a one-day retreat for myself. The one day retreat was actually a compromise. Life had gotten so overwhelming for me that I felt like dropping out of *everything* for a year.

I woke up early on my retreat day and drove to a Christian conference center about thirty miles east of Portland, Oregon. I checked into a comfortably furnished room. For very little money, it would be mine for eight hours—no radio, no television, and no people except the occasional sojourner I passed on the quiet pathway circling the conference grounds. It was a gentle autumn day, and I was quickly lost in the rich beauty of yellow and gold leaves crocheted together to form treed archways. And as they always do, the falling leaves reminded me of my own shortening days.

Reluctantly I left the golden paths and returned to my room. Three books lay open on the table—my Bible, my appointment calendar, and a blank notebook. Other than a thermos of hot apple cider spiced with cinnamon and fresh lemon, these were the only things I had brought from home. Kneeling on the thinly carpeted floor, I folded my arms across the chair, bowed my head, and began praying for God to help me get my life back in control. Seconds later I was so sleepy that I moved from the floor to the couch and drifted into a sound sleep. When I woke I didn't feel guilty at all. Instead I smiled, thinking this was part of God's answer. Rest.

Pouring a cup of hot cider, I began to list in my notebook my areas of strengths and giftedness. To help me focus, I used some of the same questions suggested in the previous chapter: What pursuits tended to bring me the most compliments? What did I feel most comfortable and confident doing? What did my friends think I was best at? What areas came most naturally to me?

I also spent a little time thinking about the end of my life—not to be morbid, but to consider what kind of legacy I wanted to leave behind. I wanted my children and grandchildren to think of me as someone other than a worn-out woman. I wanted them to look back and see a loving person who always had time for them, who made a difference for Christ in the world, who spent her short time on earth doing something that mattered. This really helped me focus on what I wanted to do with my life.

Finally, turning to a fresh page, I scribbled a heading across the top: "Longings." Then I started to write—rapidly and with abandon, not worrying that anyone other than God would read my jottings. I didn't cross out anything. Not yet.

You saw me before I was born.
Every day of my life was recorded in your book.
Every moment was laid out
before a single day had passed.
How precious are your thoughts about me, O God!
They are innumerable!

PSALM 139:16–17

Next I thoughtfully read through Psalm 139, enjoying the wonder of God's tenderness to me as I lingered over verses 16 and 17 (see previous page). Another walk in the crisp autumn air refreshed me further. Then I was ready to look again at my page of longings and narrow it down to something that might become a goal or purpose.

This was something entirely new to me. I had set goals before, but I had never really thought to connect my dreams with my goals. Goals had always been connected to what I thought I *should* do, not what I longed to do. I certainly had never stopped to think that my deep yearnings might actually be connected with God's design for my life.

I didn't want to waste time thinking about the unattainable, so it was easy to cross some items off my list. (Since I can't carry a tune, I'll never be a music diva.) Others didn't seem to line up with my season of life, my circumstances, or my strengths. Ah, but some made my heart sing. They were things I really could do (though some were a stretch!) and things I sensed would be interesting and fulfilling for me—that resonated with my sense of God's calling on my life.

It was interesting to note that these standout items were the same ones I had thought about for years but had been too busy to pursue. They were the ones on the forgotten "someday" page of my Day-Timer. Since I believe God puts dreams in our hearts, I decided I needed to pay attention when the dreams lingered.

There was still time left to look at the last piece of the

puzzle—my planner. It was time to weed out the energy drainers that did not line up with my areas of strength and God-given longings. Glancing over the entries, I noted that I was passionate about very few activities. It was easy to spot my pattern of making commitments based on what someone else wanted me to do.

For a long time I had desired to make changes in my schedule, but my retreat day changed desire into resolve. I thought about the words some wise sage had written. "To get out of the cycle will take time and hard work, but the vibrancy and joy is worth it." Then I took my pen and began to make plans for change.

Make Your Goals Work for You

- Pray.
- Write them down.
- Count the cost for keeping them.
- Make them meaningful.
- Give them priority.
- Be specific and practical.
- Ask someone to keep you accountable.
- Seek help if you struggle.
- Break them into steps.
- Reward yourself for each successful step.
- Do all you can to make them fun.
- Pray.

Some commitments I would finish—but not renew. Others I decided not to complete at all—and the decision left me exhilarated. I wrote down new goals that afternoon that related directly to my dreams—including steps of accountability that would push me to actually accomplish what I longed to do. I could hardly wait to get home and discuss them with family and friends to gain their input and perspective.

Keeping the Lamp Bright

My first one-day retreat was twelve years ago, and in the years since then the direction and habits of my life have changed remarkably. I still love responding to spontaneous requests, but these days I am more contemplative before saying yes. It feels good to say no when I believe that is the best answer. As I continue to pursue God-given longings and dreams, I feel fresh energy and a bubbling up in my spirit. I find myself humming and smiling more. Most important, I feel my lamp shining brighter.

That's not to say I never feel tired. I still face tumultuous times of intense activity, and I think that's appropriate. I agree with what Jean Fleming writes in her thoughtful book *Between Walden and the Whirlwind:* "The whirlwind is often a healthy part of following after Jesus. Certainly, a life constantly characterized by the whirlwind could indicate a problem, but a life never caught in the rush and press of activity would suggest a focus on self-preservation."[4]

Sometimes our dreams and God's purpose require us to spend short periods working very hard. But we don't need to stay that way continually—and I make a point of not doing so. Though life still gets crazy at times, the years of constant exhaustion are behind me.

About twice a year I set aside a day at home when three books lie open on a table—my Bible, my pocket planner, and a blank notebook. On one page of the notebook I write my strengths and giftedness, and on another page I list my longings. I let the tender words of Psalm 139 settle like a summer rain on my parched heart. I think about the legacy I want to leave. Then I pull out my calendar. The process of weeding out energy drainers takes less time than before but is still necessary.

I often think back to the day at the conference center and the beauty of yellow and gold leaves crocheted together to form treed archways. The falling leaves of autumn still remind me of my own shortening days.

But these days there is a difference.

These days my lamp is still burning brightly.

Something to Try

You can choose just one...

* Write a short (one page or less) obituary or memorial that sums up what you hope your legacy will be— what people will remember you for. Think of both qualities and accomplishments: *She lived out what she believed. She always had time to help someone. She made the church library a wonderful place to visit.* Keep this sheet at hand when you are writing your goals and planning your activities.

* Consider making one resolution you think you would really enjoy keeping (not one you think you *should* make). Share it with a special friend and ask her to keep you accountable for making this change in your life.

* Look ahead on your calendar and block off a day for a miniretreat. Check your telephone directory for retreat centers or call the chamber of commerce for suggestions. You can also enjoy your miniretreat at home (with family or roommates away) or even at a nearby hotel. Be sure to unplug the phone, hide the remote, and pretend your e-mail server is down.

* Visit a candle specialty shop or a unique gift store that carries pretty oil lamps. Select something lovely to place on a table or desk that will remind you to take care of yourself so you can keep your lamp burning brightly.

7

Face to the Sunshine

*Keep your face to the sunshine
and you cannot see the shadow.*

HELEN KELLER

As a toddler, Helen Keller lost her sight and hearing. But by the age of ten she had learned to speak, and by twenty-four she graduated with high honors from Radcliffe College. During her life she wrote numerous books, spoke widely, and received honorary degrees from universities all over the world.

Helen Keller was truly an accomplished woman, and what really drew people to her was her attitude. Her sunny smile was a regular feature in newsreels and magazines. Her writing inspired and uplifted everyone. She wasn't about to let painful circumstances ruin a perfectly good life.

And yes, Helen Keller was an exceptional woman. Certainly not your everyday worn-out woman. But like you, certainly she had days of frustration and discouragement.

Yet the same determined optimism that prompted Helen Keller to keep her face turned toward the sunshine can help lift you out of your worn-out doldrums. It's not a matter of always feeling great or having a naturally sunny disposition. It's certainly not a matter of denying the reality of rain. It's more about making choices about your approach to life.

Chuck Swindoll once wrote that "Life is 10 percent what happens to us and 90 percent how we respond to it. Attitude is the single most significant decision I make each day."[1] Each of us, at every moment of every day, has the opportunity to choose whether we will seek out the sunshine or squat in the shadow. And these choices will make a big difference in whether we live happy, energetic lives or just barely get by.

Researchers have found that how we think and what we think actually changes our brain chemistry and our health. In their book *Living to 100,* for instance, Drs. Margery Silver and Thomas Perls report that people with a positive attitude live longer and have an improved quality of life.[2] Having a positive outlook energizes you and draws people to you. It fosters success and increases productivity. It decreases stress and pushes away depression. It certainly can make you feel less worn out.

There are always things to complain about. All too often, Murphy's Law seems to be true: Whatever can possibly go wrong does go wrong. Troubles are real; disappointments can be devastating. But you still have the choice to believe the best and find positives in any situation. Circumstances don't have to dictate your attitude. You can rise above all the frustrations, but it takes what psychologists call an "internal locus of control." In everyday language, that means you are controlled by your decisions, not by your circumstances.

And no, that's not always easy, especially if you're a worn-out woman. If you're struggling with weariness, overload, and possibly depression, you might find it hard to believe the sunshine is still there, much less find the energy to look for it. When things look dark, thinking positive is truly an act of faith as well as an exercise of will. But if you can manage it—and we'll give you some ideas how in this chapter—we can guarantee your life can seem brighter.

Positive Strategy #1: Adjust Your Focus

The book of Proverbs states that as a person "thinks in his heart, so is he."[3] Certainly this just makes sense. If you dwell on the negative, you will tend to become negative. Likewise, if you turn toward the positive, your life will take a positive direction.

The apostle Paul tells us more specifically to focus on the positive. He even spells it out: "Whatever is true, whatever is noble, whatever is right, whatever is pure, whatever is lovely, whatever is admirable—if anything is excellent or praiseworthy—think about such things."[4]

But how do we keep our minds tuned toward all that is good and beautiful and bright? Here are some strategies that can help:

* *Filter your input.* There's no way around it. What you read, watch, and listen to—magazines, TV, movies, radio, Internet, CDs—affect the way you think and

feel. You don't have to deny reality—you probably do need to listen to the news occasionally!—but you can make decisions about what, when, and how much.

❋ *Feel your feelings, but don't depend on them.* Feelings are important but often inaccurate. You may *feel* that you are worthless. You may *feel* that God has abandoned you. But feeling those things doesn't make them true. If you learn to counter your negative feelings with words of truth, you'll find it easier to stay positive.

❋ *Put away negative thoughts.* We can't really help the thoughts that pop into our minds, but we don't have to dwell on them. Obsessing about problems and rehearsing hurts only add to the burdens we carry every day.

❋ *Meditate on truth and beauty.* This is precisely what Paul meant when he told us to "think about such things." As you meditate on beauty and truth, memorize positive Scripture, and repeat positive thoughts, chances are your attitude will improve.

❋ *Limit your complaining.* Sometimes you have to get your negative thoughts off your chest. But continually talking about negatives can actually reinforce them in your mind. Write out your problems or share them with a friend, but resist the temptation to whine.

❋ *Cultivate positive friends.* Misery might love company, but beware the tendency to feed your misery by spending too much time with miserable people. If you are a worn-out woman, you need the energy of positive people. Do what you can to put yourself in their path.

Positive Strategy #2: Cultivate Laughter in Your Life

I (Steve) love to laugh. I do it as often as I can, though not as often as I'd like. Laughter feels great; it also is contagious.

My family and I were flying home from Florida. It was a long flight, and the airline was screening sitcoms for our enjoyment. One of them had me laughing so hard that my sides hurt and my eyes were watering. I was out of control. Looking around, I saw that those around were also wrapped up in hilarity.

"This isn't that funny," my son said to me.

"Look around," I said. "Everybody else is laughing."

"But have you noticed that none of them is watching the show? They're all watching you."

Well, that was a *little* embarrassing. But not too embarrassing, because I believe in laughter. Lots of laughter. Hilarious, out-loud belly laughs. I believe it's good for you. I believe it can save your life. And if you're a worn-out woman, it can really brighten your attitude and lighten your load.

The book of Proverbs says, "A cheerful heart is good medicine,"[5] and science backs that up. A number of studies indicate that regular laughter can reduce blood pressure and heart problems. It also has a major impact on improving mental health, a sense of personal well-being, and even relationships. Marriage, parenting, and friendships have their tense moments when conflicts, hurt feelings, selfishness, and insensitivity blow up in our faces. During these times, a little laughter can help you skate across the thin ice and reach the other side.

New York Times bestselling author Paul Meyer says, "Laughter brightens our good times and lightens our heavy times."[6] We think that's a great way to put it. Laughter lifts you above the everyday stress and strain of life. It gives you a break from your exhaustion and worn-out ways. It reenergizes and rejuvenates you. Besides that, it is just plain fun. As an adult, it's too easy to take everything much more seriously than you need to. Children know how to laugh and have fun. In fact, children tend to smile or laugh an average of two hundred times a day. And in case you haven't noticed, children tend to have boundless energy.

What is so liberating about laughter? It provides a physical release for tension. It enlivens relationships and draws people together. It freshens our perspective by helping us look at life a different way. And because it's hard to take ourselves too seriously when we're laughing, a good belly laugh almost always lightens our load.

Not all laughter is healthy, of course. Cynical or derisive humor can darken our souls and feed our bitterness. But the antidote to such dark laughter is not grim-faced seriousness, but more sunshine—including lots of healthy, healing laughter. If you are feeling worn out, cultivating more laughter in your life can give you a surprising energy boost. Here are some ideas:

✳ Spend time with people who make you laugh.

✳ Seek out funny movies at your local theater or video store.

✳ Read the newspaper comics or magazine cartoons on a regular basis. If you have to, schedule this on your to-do list!

✳ Keep a humorous book or magazine in your bathroom or at your bedside. One of the main reasons I like *Reader's Digest* is that it has great humor sections.

✳ Hang out with children and animals. Not only are they inherently funny; they are masters at lighthearted, load-lifting silliness.

An old French saying asserts that "The most completely lost of all days is that on which one has not laughed." If you want to move past being worn out, we suggest you take that statement to heart. Laugh a lot.

Positive Strategy #3: Practice Gratitude

Many a motivational speaker has recommended cultivating an "attitude of gratitude." The phrase is a little corny, but the advice is sound. Deliberate gratitude has the ability to put all of life in a fresh perspective by reminding us of how blessed we truly are.

I (Steve) just spent a week with my daughter on a mission trip to Oaxacca, Mexico, working with the poorest people in that community. We laid concrete floors in small tin houses built on a garbage dump so families would not have to sleep on the dirt. One of the things that struck me was the thankfulness of the people—the family who spent the little money they had on soft drinks for us, the lady who held our hands and wept in gratitude, the man who was so giddy with excitement that his smile covered his whole face. We gave them a new floor, but they gave us a reminder of all we take for granted—the many blessings that make our lives worthwhile.

Do you remember singing that old hymn about counting your blessings?

Count your blessings, name them one by one.
Count your blessings, see what God has done.[7]

When I take the time to actually do this, I am amazed at all I am thankful for. As with eating potato chips, I can't list "just one." Once I get started, I find myself writing more and more—and feeling less and less weary. Many women even keep gratitude journals or blessing diaries in order to collect all that is good and meditate on it in the future, even sharing it with their children or grandchildren. My friend Carol keeps a file of encouraging letters and notes sent to her by family and friends. She calls it her "blush file," and she enjoys reading through it when she needs a lift.

But gratitude means more than just reminding ourselves of the good things in our lives. The whole point of counting blessings in the first place is remembering that all these good things are *gifts* from God—and saying thank You for them. We are to thank Him for the little things, the big things, and everything. In the process, we remind ourselves of the Lord's constant care for us, and that lightens our load even more.

We are even supposed to thank God in the midst of our problems, when we aren't feeling very blessed. King David did that. Even with all his troubles, he filled the book of Psalms with reminders to "Give thanks to the LORD, for he is good."[8] In the process, I believe, he helped keep his face toward the sunshine.

This is good counsel for those days when the good things in life seem to be hiding. These are the times you'll be tempted just to shrug gloomily and move to the next item on a lengthy to-do list. But let me encourage you to dig deeper.

Nancie Carmody wrote a short article in *Family Circle* magazine that did just that. She wrote that she could be thankful when the alarm clock went off "because it means I'm alive" and when her clothes fit too snugly "because it means I have enough to eat" and when there was cooking, cleaning, and fixing "because it means I have a home" and even when she was exhausted at the end of the day "...because it means I have been productive."[9]

As difficult as it may seem, you can choose to be grateful for life's challenges. In the process, you might discover you have more blessings than you realize.

I'm Thankful for...

*A*ir and autumn and animals
babies and *B*reath and beauty
children and compassion and *C*reativity
daylight and *D*ew and daffodils
*E*motions and energy and enthusiasm
faith and *F*amily and friends
grandparents and grandchildren and *G*od
hands and *H*ealth and hope
*I*ce cream and intelligence and intuition
joy and *J*ourneys and jokes
kindness and kisses and *K*ittens
love and *L*aughter and leaves
*M*others and music and memories
night and *N*ature and neighbors
order and oranges and *O*ceans
peace and *P*atience and prayer
*Q*uiet and quality and questions
rain and *R*est and romance
sunshine and smiles and *S*tars
time and *T*eachers and trees
*U*nity and understanding and uniqueness
vision and *V*alues and vacations
winter and water and *W*isdom
excitement and e*X*pression and experience
*Y*outh and yearning and yesterday
zest and *Z*ip and zeal

TAMI STEPHENS[10]

Learning to Be Content

Remember those eight items the apostle Paul told us to "think about" in Philippians 4? A few sentences later, he writes, "I have learned to be content whatever the circumstances."

That *whatever* holds the secret of a positive attitude. If you make sunshine a priority no matter what the weather, you'll live your life with a lot more energy. The higher you look, the better you will feel. So adjust your focus on the brightest and laugh out loud and count your blessings.

And through it all, remember that God is an optimist. He knows your great potential—and with Him all things are possible. As you keep that in mind, life gets exciting, and doors of wonder open all around you. Albert Einstein put it this way: "There are only two ways to live your life: One is as though nothing is a miracle. The other is as though everything is a miracle."

I don't know about you, but I'm choosing the miracle.

Something to Try

You can choose just one...

※ Think about the most positive person you know. How does that person deal with various challenges that come his or her way?

※ Share with someone one of the following:

The funniest joke you have heard.

The funniest situation you have been in.

The funniest movie you have seen.

The comic strip you think is the funniest.

The funniest person you have ever met.

※ Take the night off and rent that favorite funniest movie. Don't just smile or chuckle, but laugh out loud at all the funny parts.

※ For the next five nights, write down five specific blessings before you go to sleep. (Try for a different set of blessings each night.) Read them to yourself first thing when you wake up.

8

Yellow Umbrellas

Kindness is a yellow umbrella
covering the rainy days of life.

KIMBER ANNE ENGSTROM

W e know, we know. You don't want to hear about one more thing to do. Your accumulated list already exceeds your life expectancy! But what if there was something that takes hardly any time at all? Something that makes you and others incredibly happy? Something perfect for the worn-out woman because it invigorates instead of depleting?

Sound too good to be true? It's not.

Back in 1982, a woman named Anne Herbert had an idea. She scribbled it on a placemat in a Sausalito, California, restaurant: "Practice random acts of kindness and senseless acts of beauty." Some years later, a professor named Chuck Wall apparently came up with the idea independently—his phrase was "random acts of senseless kindness"—and challenged his college classes to put it into action. The idea caught on and circled the globe. There were books, organizations, magazine articles, newspaper reports, and bumper stickers that said, "Honk if you love random acts of kindness." Oprah Winfrey devoted entire shows to the idea. A movie called *Pay It Forward* dramatized the possibilities. And February 17 became recognized by many as Random Acts of Kindness Day.

The best part of all this is that "random acts of kindness" became much more than just a slogan. People actually started being kind and compassionate, and the ripple effect was astounding. One sixth-grade student whose class had committed to doing ten thousand spontaneous good deeds in one month summed up the excitement: "When I do something for somebody else, I feel really happy."

It's hard to sprinkle sunshine on others without getting some on yourself.

Practicing random acts of kindness provides an excellent pick-me-up for the worn-out woman. It doesn't ask you to hurry faster or commit to a long-term project. It simply asks you to slow down enough to be aware of your surroundings and to respond spontaneously. Instead of making you feel more tired, it creates energy and joy.

It's true what Jesus said: "You're far happier giving than getting."[1] Giving doesn't have to mean big spending or a long-term commitment. It's surprising how even a tiny act of thoughtfulness and generosity can make a huge difference in another person's life.

A little praise. A little encouragement. A little act of thoughtfulness. You'll find a little goes a long, long way.

Practicing Random Kindness—Some Ideas

Let someone cut in front of you. ✦ Give a larger tip than usual. ✦ Take flowers to the hospital and ask the nurse to deliver them to a patient who doesn't have any. ✦ Offer to return the grocery cart for an elderly person or a mother with small children. ✦ Send a thank-you note to someone who doesn't expect it. ✦ Take blankets to a homeless shelter or an animal shelter. ✦ Send a gift anonymously. ✦ Compliment five people in an afternoon. ✦ Donate to a worthy cause. ✦ Help without being asked. ✦ Buy a bunch of daisies and pass them out to people you pass on the sidewalk. ✦ Send a valentine to a widow. ✦ Write a note of encouragement to a teenager. ✦ Make someone new feel welcome. ✦ Run an errand for someone who is sick. ✦ Let someone know you are praying for him or her.

A Little Praise

For years I (Alice) battled a critical spirit. It seemed to be my mission in life to notice what was wrong and make sure someone heard about it. What a draining lifestyle! Finally I made a commitment to start noticing what was right and telling others. That was much more fun.

When I'm at a shopping mall, for instance, I intentionally look around for employees who sweep or pick up clutter. I walk up and say something like, "If it wasn't for you, I wouldn't shop here." I pause just long enough for them to think I'm a bit weird and then continue: "I can't imagine what this place would look like without you. You're doing a great job. I really appreciate what you do." It's fun to watch the workers' expressions change. I walk away with a bounce in my step because I've made someone feel better about his or her job.

A little praise can work wonders with families, too. My children and grandchildren have thrived since I learned to hand out praise in place of so much criticism.

In *Leaving the Light On,* John Trent tells a beautiful story about a little girl who is feeling out of sorts. One Saturday morning the dad tells his little girl that he wants to take her on a date at her favorite restaurant—she can choose. Within an hour, they're sliding into a booth at McDonald's. Before they start in on their foam platters of eggs and pancakes, the dad takes his little girl's hand and tells her how thankful he is that she belongs to their family. He uses words like *treasure* and *precious,* and he points out some specific things about her that he loves.

When the father finally picks up his fork to start eating, the little girl pushes his hand back down and softly pleads, "Longer, daddy...longer." So once again he takes her hand and tells her how much she means to him. Three more times he hears, "Longer, daddy...longer" and complies. Then, when they finally get home, he hears her skip into the kitchen and announce to her mom,

"Guess what! I'm special. Daddy told me so."[2]

Everywhere we go, people are longing to feel that they are special because someone told them so. You can be that person. Whether you are a stay-at-home mom, own your company, or work for minimum wage, your words of praise can change a life—and often they will bounce back to you. They will give you a lift and make your heart sing. Because you care enough to give out a little praise, you're special, too.

Kind words can be
short and easy to speak,
but their echoes are truly endless.

MOTHER TERESA

A Little Encouragement

Encouragement is just as important as praise. I know I love it when people encourage me. Even a few words can help me out of a blue mood or calm my frustrations. And I've found that speaking words of encouragement to someone else can be a surefire spirit lifter.

When people share their hopes and dreams with you, be the one to point out the wonderful possibilities. Plenty of others will point out the problems.

As busy women, we are sometimes reluctant to give encouragement because then we feel obligated to get involved and take on the other person's challenges. But encouragement doesn't mean doing other people's work or making their dreams come true. It doesn't mean becoming one person's full-time cheerleader. There are simple ways to encourage that take very little time—pointing out a child's talent or capability, reminding a discouraged friend of the successes she has already achieved, or helping a teen articulate the next few steps needed to reach her goals. Just listening intently with words like "tell me more" can be an encouragement. So can a gentle nudge to urge someone to do what she needs to do.

A Little Act of Thoughtfulness

It seems odd, but doing spontaneous little deeds gives me more fulfillment than long-term achievements. It's a quick way to fill up when my emotional tank is empty. My heart is still smiling, in fact, about something that happened several years ago.

Since I enjoy fresh flowers but don't have a garden, it's a nice treat to pick up bouquets at the grocery store. A bunch of mixed flowers costs less than five dollars where I shop, and they stay fresh for more than a week. I love it! One Friday when I was picking out my bouquet, I felt a little tap on my heart that seemed to say *Buy two*. It was just a feeling, one that could easily be ignored. But I chose a second bouquet anyway.

When I got to the checkout line, I pulled my cart in behind an elderly lady. She was less than five feet tall, very tidy, and seemed quite organized about her purchases. As the clerk finished bagging her few items, I had a second nudge on my heart. *The flowers are for her.* She was already walking away, and so I grabbed one of the bouquets, told the clerk to ring me up for two, and said I'd be back in a second.

Coming up from behind, I spoke softly so I wouldn't startle the little lady. "Excuse me, but I think God wants you to have these flowers." When she turned around, her wrinkled face was a wonder—tears gathering in the deep creases of her smile.

"Oh, my, I don't know what to say," she stammered. "What a lovely gift. My husband always used to bring me flowers, but I haven't had any since he died more than four years ago. Today I was struggling with memories and feeling lonely. You'll never know how much this means to me."

I'll always remember that moment when God let me be part of His surprise. Every once in a while I still like buying two bouquets and listening for a little tap on my heart that says, *The flowers are for her.*

On days when you are feeling negative and irritable or just plain worn out, let the simple pleasure of doing random deeds of kindness lift your spirit. It's like giving yellow umbrellas to cover the rainy days of life.

Something to Try

You can choose just one...

- Sometime this week, when you are at a store or restaurant, find at least two people you can compliment for their service.

- Think of someone you know who may need encouragement. Within the next twenty-four hours, make a call or send a note.

- Look at the list of suggested acts of kindness on page 101. Add a few ideas of your own to the list. Then ask a friend to compete with you to see how many items you can do in one month.

- Make a double batch of bath salts using the following recipe. Keep some for yourself and give the rest away. *Place 3 cups Epsom salts in a large bowl. In a measuring cup, combine 1 tablespoon glycerin, a couple of drops of food coloring, and a spray of your favorite perfume. Mix well. Slowly add the liquid mixture to the Epsom salts, stirring well to combine. Pour the mixture into decorative glass jars and tie on a ribbon bow.*[3]

9

The Secret
of Simplicity

*Simplicity is the dream
of all who have too much to do.*

UNKNOWN

ow did life get so complicated and cluttered? Anne asked herself.

She looked around at her large house, her busy schedule, her worries and concerns, and realized she had lost herself. Her life was too unfocused, too fast, too full. She had to get away in order to clear her mind and catch her breath. So Anne spent two weeks alone at the beach in a small cottage with no electricity. Each day she watched the waves and walked in the sand and wrote in her journal.

From this experience Anne Morrow Lindbergh wrote an amazing little book called *Gift from the Sea.* In its early pages she eloquently describes the disconnect between intentions and reality that frustrates so many worn-out women: "I mean to lead a simple life.... But I do not. I find that my frame of life does not foster simplicity. It does not bring peace, it destroys the soul."[1]

But over the course of her seaside stay, Anne Morrow Lindbergh came to understand the serene secret to truly enjoying life. It is figuring out "how little one can get along with, not how much."

The secret, in other words, is simplicity.

The trouble is that achieving simplicity is not always that simple.

We all have a haunting ache for a simpler life with fewer complications, more peace, more joy, more freedom. Yet we also have an addictive attraction to *more*. We live our lives right in the middle of too much—too much information, too much noise, too much activity, too much *stuff*. Our clutter suffocates us. It blocks us and distracts us, weighs us down and trips us up. Yet we keep collecting it, stuffing it in, filling our minds with it, scheduling it, piling it in corners and on countertops, stashing it in cars and handbags. Sometimes we even borrow other people's clutter.

Most of us believe that simplifying is part of the cure for our weary reality, but we don't know where to begin. We're not even sure we know what is extraneous and what is necessary.

As we said, simplifying isn't always simple! (But it's worth it.)

To achieve the goal of uncluttering your life, your simplifying efforts need to encompass at least three areas—your soul, your schedule, and your physical space. In each area, the same basic plan can guide your efforts.

We've outlined it in the sidebar below. In the rest of this chapter, we'll look more specifically at how you can simplify each area of life.

A Simple Plan for Simplifying Your Life

* *Pray it out.* Start by committing the whole simplification project to God.

* *Parcel it out.* Unless you have a big chunk of time on your hands, we suggest you focus your simplifying efforts on one area of your life—one drawer, one room, one month, one issue—at a time.

* *Ask someone to help you out.* You can use some support for making hard decisions about what to keep and what not to.

* *Sort it out.* Once you start, address one item after another and decide what to do with it—confess it, delegate it, talk about a feeling, cancel it, file it, give it away.

* *Carry out* your decisions right away—before you proceed to something else. If you can't do it on the spot, mark your calendar. If it's a physical item, *don't* put it back where you got it!

* *Maintain from here on out.* Establish a plan for handling new information, new time demands, new material acquisitions.

Simplifying Your Soul

King David cried out, "Create in me a clean heart, O God."[2] Surely one way God does this is by helping us clear out the mental, emotional, and spiritual clutter we're so tired of wading through.

- *Mental* clutter involves an overload of ideas and images, issues to consider, quandaries to puzzle over, threats to worry about. You literally have "too much on your mind," and this mental clutter can lead to distractions, obsessions, or impure thoughts.

- *Emotional* clutter mostly consists of unprocessed, unresolved, and sometimes unrecognized feelings—fears, insecurities, anger, anxiety. When your life is full of emotional clutter, you probably feel confused and anxious much of the time. Anger may flare unexpectedly. You have a sense of being on the edge or out of control.

- *Spiritual* clutter has mostly to do with unrecognized and unconfessed sin in your life. Attitudes of defiance, greed, dishonesty, anger, jealousy, bitterness, lack of love, pride, lust, or selfish ambition may crowd your heart—especially if you haven't kept current with God.

Soul clutter is the most damaging of all clutter. Not only can it wear you down and burn you out; it can destroy all that is meaningful to you and those you love. Take care of your soul and all else will become clearer. With such soul simplicity, stress has fewer corners in which to hide.

In our experience, the best strategy for uncluttering the soul involves a pen, a piece of paper, and some time on our knees. Writing down thoughts and feelings helps us sort them all out so we can make the right decisions. A trusted friend or counselor can also be a tremendous help in making necessary decisions.

Taking our confused thoughts and feelings to God in prayer also helps us sort out the junk and focus our thinking. Prayer provides the God-ordained answer to spiritual clutter. Confessing sin, expressing repentance, asking for and accepting God's forgiveness—this process is the spiritual equivalent to cleaning out the cluttered closet that's driving us crazy. (We'll have more to say about this in chapter 13.)

Simplifying Your Schedule

Comedian Steven Wright says, "I think God is going to come down and pull civilization over for speeding." He's got a point. Most of us move far too fast, and we pack our schedules with no margin for error. At this pace it becomes difficult, if not impossible, to discover and appreciate all the things in life that really matter. As you race to reach your goals or obligations or to just keep up, true joy becomes a nice thought and nothing more.

The faster you go, the more you tend to skim the surface of your life instead of going deep. You do what is quick and expedient, not necessarily what is important. You listen in sound bites, grab meals on the run, exercise when you can fit it in, and produce only what is demanded. Such a lifestyle fills time without filling you as a person, leaving you relationally, emotionally, and spiritually superficial. Uncluttering your schedule slows you down and gives you the time to grow deep and to enjoy life.

Stu and Tauni did this in a drastic way when they decided to quit their high-paying, prestigious jobs and sell their large suburban home. Tauni explained that her lifestyle was destroying her health and her marriage. "We are so busy earning money and running about that we don't have time to live." So they bought a much smaller house out in the country, got less demanding jobs, and learned to slow down. "This was one of the best things we've ever done," said Tauni. "Now I have time to relax and love and live."

You may not be ready to take that big a step just to unclutter your schedule. But I can promise you any efforts you make at clearing your "schedule clutter" can clear out a lot of stress as well. In chapter 6, Alice describes a time when she did just that and suggests a helpful strategy for regular "calendar cleaning."

Simplifying Your Space

Our culture is obsessed with stuff. It occupies our days and dreams. We love getting it, though it rarely satisfies for very long. Stuff often seems to own us as much as we own it. Most of us have far more than we need, but we still have a hard time resisting the urge to add more to the accumulation.

Jesus spoke very pointedly to this issue—and the limitations of a stuff-centered existence: "Don't store up treasures here on earth, where they can be eaten by moths and get rusty, and where thieves break in and steal."[3] We collect stuff and clutter because it gives us a false sense of security, comfort, and pride. But that's a deception. In reality physical clutter gives us disorder, stress, and more work.

The More You Have

THE MORE YOU HAVE, the more you want.

THE MORE YOU HAVE, the less you're satisfied.

THE MORE YOU HAVE, the more people will come after it.

THE MORE YOU HAVE, the more you realize it does you no good.

THE MORE YOU HAVE, the more you have to worry about.

THE MORE YOU HAVE, the more you can hurt yourself by holding on to it.

THE MORE YOU HAVE, the more you have to lose.

THE MORE YOU HAVE, the more you'll leave behind.

RANDY ALCORN[4]

To combat physical clutter, we suggest you target a room or even a part of a room, pick up each item, and ask the following questions: Do I need it? Do I enjoy it? Does it really matter? Have I used it in the past year? If you can't say yes to at least one of these questions, it may be time to let it go. If you can't bring yourself to throw or give things away, put them in a box with a six-month date on the outside and reconsider at that time. When you bring something new into your space, try your best to get rid of something else.

And if all of this seems like more than you can handle, we urge you to get some help. A good book on home organization[5] can provide direction. An honest friend or even a professional organizer can help you make those hard decisions. Any investment of time or money you make now in the service of simplicity will more than pay for itself in peace and renewed energy.

The Freedom of Simplicity

Only a few things are necessary. Having too much steals the life from our souls and distracts us from the most important aspects of life. When we choose simplicity, the blindfold of being worn out is lifted and we begin to see with new eyes the wonders that surround us.

A teacher asked her young students to make a list of the seven natural wonders of the world. Most of the children finished their lists quickly and then ran outside to enjoy recess. Only one little girl remained at her desk thinking about what to write. Suddenly she smiled, wrote something, handed her paper to her teacher, and skipped happily outside to play with the others. The teacher turned the paper over and read the following:

Seeing

Hearing

Tasting

Touching

Running

Laughing

Loving

Quite simply...who could ask for more?

Something to Try

You can choose just one...

* To help unclutter your mind, try an audiovisual fast (no television, radio, CD player, or computer) for twenty-four hours. When you are finished, write down how you feel about the experiment.

* Walk around your home with a basket or bag. Gather several items you are willing to give away. Take your bag immediately to your car and drive to the nearest thrift store or charitable drop box.

* If you were to write down seven things you consider "wonders," what would be on your list?

* Imagine the simple pleasure of standing at the edge of the surf on a sandy beach with your back to the water as the surf runs out. Doesn't it feel like you're traveling backward, even though you are standing still? That's a wonder, isn't it?

10

Soul Nurturing

The LORD is my shepherd;
I have everything I need.
He lets me rest in green meadows;
he leads me beside peaceful streams.

PSALM 23:1–3

don't the words of Psalm 23 give a beautiful picture of a peaceful, soul-nurturing time? Doesn't your worn-out spirit yearn for such a tranquil time with your Lord—resting in green meadows, strolling beside peaceful streams or "still waters," as the old familiar *King James Version* puts it?

Janey, who recently retired, is learning anew the joys of walking beside still waters. "It is my habit to wake up early and spend time curled up in a cozy chair on the sunrise side of the house. With open Bible, this is my time to reflect, to pray...and to dream. These moments of solitude are a pleasant way to welcome the treasure of a new day."

But Barbara, a mother of toddlers, has a different view of mornings: "Yes, I hear it, but I can't believe it's morning already. The alarm sounds thick and far away. My arms are at anchor and my eyelids are stubbornly half-mast. Six o'clock and already the day's not adding up: Although I went to bed at eleven, I feel like I've only gotten a few hours sleep."

Eve, a career woman, comments that she understands why the alarm clock has such an awful name. The second the alarm goes off, she bolts out of bed and starts multi-tasking her day. She eats on the run, checks her voice messages while she dresses, and sends up arrow prayers when she's stuck in traffic.

Can it be true that the simple pleasure of being alone with our thoughts and our God is reserved only for those with uncluttered schedules like Janey? In his book *Margin*, Dr. Richard Swenson asks, "Doesn't God lead people beside still waters anymore?"[1] Many worn-out women would echo the question. We don't truly believe that God has suddenly become pro-exhaustion, but sometimes we feel He hasn't given us *enough* time to follow Him to still waters.

But the problem isn't with God, of course. We can't even put all the blame for the parched condition of our worn-out souls on our hyped-up culture. The Lord still calls us to follow Him beside still waters on a regular basis so He can restore us. But He never forces us to do what is good for us. When He calls, we have to follow.

I (Alice) believe that women intuitively understand the value of soul nurturing, which is what happens when we follow the Lord's leading. When our need for such nurture is left untended, the longing for it deepens. We are like the deer that King David wrote about:

As the deer pants for streams of water,
so my soul pants for you, O God.[2]

Even if we are in a season of life where we are barely
hanging on, our souls' deep thirst—plus the Lord's leading
and a little ingenuity— can help us find a way to welcome
God into our day.

Find Time to Nurture Your Soul

Barbara Curtis, the mother of toddlers mentioned earlier,
writes about her experience as a young mom and new
Christian: "One day, as I was unrolling a multitude of
balled-up socks for the washer, I prayed, *Lord, is there a
prayer closet somewhere for me? And what about this thing
they call quiet time?*" The Lord gave her an answer that was
wordlessly impressed upon her heart: "Aren't you praying
now?" Barbara continues, "And so my laundry room
became my prayer closet. This is where I meet the Lord
each morning before my children wake and at intervals
throughout the day as I transfer clothes from baskets to
washer, from washer to dryer, and from dryer to baskets
again. In these twelve- and twenty-minute snatches, I have
found my quiet time."[3]

Eve, the one who relates to the awful name for alarm
clocks, is good at keeping scheduled appointments. She discovered that something as simple as writing "time with
God" on her calendar was a turning point for her. By giving

these appointments the same priority she gives other important matters, Eve feels less harried and these days enjoys more of a sense of harmony.

Rhonda Byrd works with women in leadership at her church. Last December, each woman had a calendar for the upcoming year and individually took time at the meeting to schedule special "date times" with the Lord once a month. These special date times last one hour and are in addition to daily devotions or Bible study. Rhonda says, "Try scheduling something on your calendar and then canceling on Jesus!"

Rhonda describes one of her special "Jesus dates" this way: "I sent my husband and toddler son out for pizza, and I stayed home and walked around thanking the Lord for just being HIM! I had candles burning and my favorite praise and worship CD playing low and softly in the background."[4]

For many people, exercise provides a wonderful opportunity for quiet time. While the body is working, the mind and spirit are free to commune with the Lord, and the very act of working out provides a form of solitude. In spite of an extraordinary ministry that took them to all parts of the world, Norman Vincent Peale and his wife, Ruth, found a way to find solitude, even when they were exercising together. For many years, they took a daily two- to three-mile walk together, but they did not speak. They called it "their alone time together."

Finding time to nurture your soul is a unique quest for

each person. You might want to try one of the ideas mentioned above, reworking it to fit your situation, or come up with a totally different way all your own. God is still leading beside the still waters, and He will help you find the time to follow.

Faith is...
Resting in His love,
His presence,
His provision.

PAMELA REEVE[5]

Find a Pleasant Place

Once you've found the time to nurture your soul, find a place. It doesn't have to be the same place every day, but I think nurturing places need to feel restful—like pillows of serenity. They need to be peaceful, welcoming, comfortable—places that by their very nature foster quiet contentment.

Anita says her soul is nurtured when she walks through her garden, observing the beauty of all its stages (even before or after the blooming). Sometimes Allison's pleasant place is as simple as sitting beside a bouquet of hyacinths, enjoying the scent of their perfume. Carol enjoys relaxing on the deck in her backyard, watching robins bathing in the birdbath, her dog curled up at her feet.

Others describe their pleasant places as a front-porch swing, a cozy corner in a favorite room, at the kitchen table drinking coffee from a well-loved cup, an early morning walk along a tree-lined street, or a lazy afternoon by the sea. Some people love to find a corner in a quiet coffee shop that lets them linger or even a cozy corner in a library.

If you can't *think* of a pleasant place that is easy and accessible, finding one is a "must" for your to-do list, as an investment in future tranquillity. You can create your own place as easily as lighting a fragrant candle or setting a rose on a table where you read. Or take an afternoon to clear out a corner of your bedroom or attic, and add what you need to make it comfortable and beautiful—an overstuffed chair, a throw, a little table for your books, perhaps a portable CD player.

Once you reach your pleasant place, take full advantage of its capacity to nurture your soul. Breathe in deeply, hold your breath for a few moments, and then exhale slowly. Repeat this several times. Return often to your pleasant places, and enjoy the soul-nurturing joy of just being there.

Learn to Linger

After finding times and places to welcome God into all your days—really, into all your moments—discover ways to linger so you can sink deep in His love. Kathy Callahan-Howell writes that this can be "like throwing a rock in the pond and waiting for the ripples to settle. It takes some time to settle ourselves and be still before God."[6]

If you have to-do lists longer than there are hours in the day, you may find it hard to linger with the Lord for even fifteen minutes. While you are trying to settle yourself before God, your mind may be distracted, busily working on your lists. You may feel like the productivity police will come knocking at your door if you linger for more than a few moments. Other women who have experienced this same frustration have found some of the following ideas helpful:

A Corner to Prepare

Keep all your quiet-time materials in one place. My little treasure corner has a Bible, a devotional book, a journal, a pretty notepad, favorite bookmarks, and two pens—one for highlighting and one for writing. The notepad is a place for jotting down errands or phone calls that come to mind while I'm trying to linger. I find that writing them down takes away their distracting power. My friend Sharon keeps her "treasure corner" in a pretty little basket. She says that way she can easily transport it to wherever she chooses: the porch swing, her favorite chair, or even a back table at her favorite coffee shop.

A Page to Read

Whether you are reading it through in a year or only a few verses a day, devote part of your time to reading the Bible. Joanna Bloss, in a magazine article entitled

"Spiritually Dry," suggests studying Psalm 119 for a month. Read just six verses each day, and write down the blessings and benefits of knowing God's Word.[7] Reading from a devotional book is another great way to nourish your spirit. We've listed some classics and a few of our current favorites in the recommended reading section at the back of this book.

A Conversation to Share

Prayer is not a monologue but a conversation. Pray as though God is present. (He is!) Instead of praying at fast-forward speed, have quiet moments when you listen. One of my favorite ways of praying is to pause briefly after each statement of praise, each request, and listen for how God responds. When I praise Him for His attributes, I sense His pleasure. When I share my deepest worries, I hear in my heart comforting words such as, *Trust Me, My child. Your loved one is never out of my care.*

> There is time in which to be, simply be,
> that time in which God quietly tells us who we are
> and who he wants us to be.
> It is then that God takes our emptiness
> and fills it with what he wants.
>
> MADELEINE L'ENGLE

124

If you are a woman on the run, it is likely you start your quiet time with prayer petitions and may be out of time before you get to praise. You can develop a new dimension in your soul-nurturing time by sometimes reversing the order. In her book *Legacy of a Pack Rat,* Ruth Bell Graham tells about her routine of getting up early, fixing a cup of coffee, and then sitting in the rocker on the front porch, where she prayed for each of their children and grandchildren. One morning she got up earlier than usual, and before she began her prayers she listened to the waking of the dawn. She described it as a symphony, the air liquid with music as if the whole creation was praising God at the beginning of a new day. She ends by saying, "And I learned a lesson. I had been beginning my days with petitions, and I should have been beginning them with praise."[8]

 A Journal to Keep

Many of the godly women I know keep journals. Some write in them every single day, and others write only now and then. You might find it rewarding to keep a blank notebook or journal with you during your quiet time so that when God speaks to you through Scripture or during your prayer time, you can write down what you hear so you won't forget.

A journal can be as simple as a spiral notebook or as elegant as a tapestry-covered book sold with a *real* fountain pen. Shopping for a journal is always a pleasant time for me. I like to find one with lined pages and a pretty cover that looks inviting in my "treasure corner." I'm a sporadic journal writer, but I love rereading thoughts and prayers from other years. Woven through the pages are Scripture verses written out in longhand, where I've added a little heart and the words *God's promise*. There are pages where I've been morbidly sad, fiercely angry, or incredibly happy. Other pages are best described as love letters to God. When I look back at my journals, my own words inspire me to journal more often. (Perhaps, after writing this, I will.)

Time Out for Soul Nurturing

These ideas are only beginning steps. There is so much more to soul nurturing. Chapters 6 and 18 will give you more ideas and may inspire you to plan small retreats for your soul.

And make no mistake—soul nurturing is not optional. It's not a luxury, but a necessity. I could almost define the worn-out woman as a person who has allowed her soul to parch and wither because, for one reason or another, she has not been able to spend time beside still waters. None of us can find balance in our lives or become the women God has in mind for us to be if there is no room for the quietness that restores our souls.

The good news, of course, is that God *wants* us to have time with Him. He will lead us beside still waters if we just make it a priority to listen and follow.

In her writing, Carole Mayhall often delights me with her insight and the beauty of her observations. The following excerpt reminds us that it is often in quiet moments of reflection that we discover the simple wonders that refresh us:

It was a pristine, state-of-the-art spring day in Washington State—snow-capped mountains, sparkling bays, brilliant flowers. Driving along a picturesque country road, we passed a well-groomed farm with a trim rail fence and saw a neatly lettered sign that said:

PLEASE DRIVE QUIETLY

Some music notes followed the letters. We puzzled over the meaning until we spied another sign fifty yards further. Trailed by more music notes, it read:

MEADOWLARKS SINGING.[9]

Something to Try

You can choose just one...

✦ Think about some of the pleasant places where you like to spend quiet moments. Describe one of your favorites. Better yet, *go* there right now.

✦ For one month, try the idea suggested by Joanna Bloss: Read just six verses each day from Psalm 119, and write down the blessings and benefits of knowing God's Word.

✦ Find a friend or family member who will agree to ask you the following question every day for one week: "How did you nurture your soul today?"

✦ Spend some time browsing through journals at a bookstore or stationery store. Enjoy the variety and beauty of the exterior artwork. Feel the texture of the cover and the pages. Notice that some have ribbon markers, others spiral binding. Some are lined for ease of writing; some are unlined to invite drawing as well as writing. Does the interior have inspirational quotations or artwork? If you just fall in love with one, consider buying it even if you have never journaled before.

11

You Gotta Have Friends

A true friend shares freely, advises wisely,
assists willingly, encourages quickly,
takes all patiently, defends courageously,
and continues a friend unchangeably.

ADAPTED FROM WILLIAM PENN

When Sally discovered her husband was having an affair, her life shattered. She was hurt and angry and scared. She felt like a failure as a wife and didn't know what to do next. She felt alone in her pain but was anxious about what people would think if she shared her problem with anyone. For days she carried her secret alone, trying to hide the despair that filled every hour of life.

But at a morning Bible study, a good friend greeted her with a hug and asked, "Sally, how are you doing?" The dam broke. Tears came faster than Sally could wipe them away. Her dear friend guided her to a private corner and gently whispered, "I'd love to listen."

Sally opened her heart and told her story. When she finished, the friend softly placed her arm around Sally's shoulder and said, "I won't say I know how you feel, but I know it hurts. And I promise you that no matter how long it takes I'll be here. I'll stand beside you whenever you need me."

Sharing her heartbreak with a trusted friend and hearing those words of support gave Sally the glimmer of hope she so desperately needed. It's the same hope that every worn-out woman needs.

No matter how much you enjoy other people, being worn out can make you isolate yourself from others. The higher your level of stress, exhaustion, or depression, the more you tend to retreat. Yet this is the very time you need people the most—not just anybody, of course, but trustworthy friends who can make a good support system. You need them for at least five different reasons.

Friends Provide Perspective

When you are overwhelmed, it's easy to get stuck and not see all of your options. Sometimes the answers to your stress and struggles are right in front of you, but you need some assistance to find them. Friends can give you that assistance. They can keep you balanced or help you regain your balance. No matter how intelligent or capable you are, there will be days you feel lost, when you need some clear direction, some fresh ideas, or just a different perspective. And again, that's what friends are for.

Places to Find a Friend

🌼 *Find a cause.* Get involved in a worthwhile project that tugs at your heart. You'll find people there with a similar heart. And you'll accomplish something meaningful in the midst of your friendship hunt.

🌼 *Find a church.* Get plugged into a church that believes as you do. Be sure you make it to the small groups and the extra activities offered for your age group—even if you're shy.

🌼 *Find a class.* Aerobics, crafts, and college-credit courses all offer a place to meet people with common interests, which makes it easier to strike up conversation and build a friendship.

🌼 *Find a club.* Play groups and other organized functions for children can help you find friends while your kids do, too.

🌼 *Find a committee.* If you have good leadership skills, jumping into a job in a church or civic organization is a wonderful way to connect. Working side by side with people can forge close friendships while accomplishing a worthy objective.

RHONDA RHEA[1]

131

Friends Provide Company

Being a worn-out woman is a lonely experience. You might be surrounded by people, but they seem far away. At times it feels as if no one understands or even cares about you. Though you might long for friends, connecting with them might seem like too much work.

Once you reach out, however, you find that good company is as refreshing as a barefoot walk on the beach.

Good company provides a distraction from the pressures of your day, comfort from the hurts of life, and escape from the loneliness. Trusted friends know when to give you space and when to come close. They walk with you and stand by you. Friends take the time to learn how to love you, and as that famous passage in 1 Corinthians says, they show you love that "endures through every circumstance"[2] (even your worn-out state). Sometimes friends *laugh* with you and sometimes they *cry* with you, but most importantly, friends are always willing to *be* with you.

132

Friends Provide a Place to Vent

Every day a host of difficulties presses down on you. Some days you can handle it; other days you just have to let it all out. Sometimes you need a shoulder to cry on. Other times you need a willing ear to listen to your rants and raves. Then there are times when you just feel like complaining about the injustices and annoyances that fill this world. Some of these complaints are significant and some are trivial, but sometimes you just need to get them out of your system.

The opposite of venting, often called "stuffing," is one of the fastest ways to increase your stress and become a worn-out woman. Stuffing means that you ignore your fears, frustrations, and other negative feelings, pushing them so far down that you don't even feel them anymore—until they erupt in the form of an inappropriate outburst, a compulsive behavior such as overeating, or even a serious health problem.

Venting to a good friend can be a lifesaver, but it's important to choose that friend carefully. Some people won't understand that you're just letting off steam and will step in and try to solve your problem. Some aren't trustworthy and will share what you said with other people. Some might take your ranting personally or exaggerate it beyond your intent.

Even if you're sure your listener is understanding and trustworthy, it's a good idea to let her know when you are about to vent. Then she'll understand what you need—her patient, nonjudgmental listening.

133

One final word about confiding in others about your problems: Although there will be men in your larger circle of friends, your closest confidants should be women. Too often affairs begin because women turn to male friends who appear to be better listeners than their husbands. Even if you're not married, confiding your deepest secrets to a male friend can create a sense of intimacy that sends the wrong signal or gets a relationship off to a false start. If you are married, venting to your female friends can help take some of the strain off your relationship with your husband—especially if you're venting about him!

Friends Provide Accountability

Let's face it: Worn-out women can sometimes be our own worst enemies. We make choices that intensify our stress, then either brag about everything we are doing or bemoan how trapped and victimized we feel. Half the time, we're just distracted and confused. And even when we commit to reforming our worn-out ways, we backslide very easily.

The more worn out you get, therefore, the more you need others to check out your thinking. A good mentor or accountability group can be a priceless asset. And if you're sure you don't have time to meet with someone in this way—that's a good sign you really need to!

To be accountable is to consent to being watched and questioned. You share with others what wears you out, letting them know those obvious and less obvious challenges that steal your energy. You also give them permission to ask questions:

- How worn out are you?
- What area of stress are you in denial about?
- Who are you most concerned about and why?
- What do you use to emotionally escape?
- When have you said yes when you should have said no?
- What bad habits have you fallen into this week?

Allowing yourself to be this transparent and vulnerable is a wonderful protection against temptation and naïveté.

You allow others to come to your aid when you've gotten yourself in a problem situation. You let them catch you when you fall and lift you back to the place where you know you should be.

Sometimes you just need to swallow your pride and trust those who care about you. They know you'll be there to do the same for them.

Friends Provide Encouragement

Worn-out women often get wrapped up in negativity and self-doubt. They might go through phases when they question their competency, value, and purpose. This is when they need someone who will come alongside them with a compliment, a hug, or just an I-believe-in-you attitude. What it all comes down to is this: When you are overwhelmed, you need at least one cheerleader.

When you are worn out and weary, it is easy to lose hope. The frustrations of the past haunt you, the stress of the present overwhelms you, and the prospect of the future discourages you. But with a support system of one or more people who genuinely care, it's amazing how much brighter the world can look.

King Solomon put it this way:

Two people can accomplish more than twice as much as one.... If one person falls, the other can reach out and help. But people who are alone when

135

they fall are in real trouble.... A person standing alone can be attacked and defeated, but two can stand back-to-back and conquer. Three are even better, for a triple-braided cord is not easily broken.[3]

The Right Kind of Friend

Friends can help you survive the worn-out, overwhelmed, and I've-had-enough moments of life. If you're a worn-out woman, friends aren't a luxury, but a necessity. But what do you do if you don't have that kind of friend in your life?

The place to start is on your knees. If you don't have that special friend or healthy support system, begin praying that God will help you find one. (Remember that God knows your needs and will take care of you, even in this area.) You can help the process along by making yourself available for friendship, even if it means paring down your schedule to make room for friends. (See chapters 6 and 9 for some tips on how to do this.) Look for kindred spirits in the midst of your many activities, and don't be afraid to make the first move. Sometimes all it takes is an invitation to share a cappuccino at the neighborhood Starbucks or a sack lunch in the park.

When you're looking for friends, keep an eye out for people who...

❋ share your faith and values,
❋ know how to listen,

* believe the best in you,

* possess a positive attitude,

* keep confidences,

* accept you and your differences,

* communicate honestly and directly,

* take the time to be there.

These are the people who will help move you quickly and compassionately out of your stress and then happily into the rest of your life. But only if you let them.

Kelly was great at her job and was highly respected by all her coworkers. When she was called into her boss's office, she honestly expected a promotion or a raise. But that was not what happened.

Her boss was furious with her. He yelled at her and accused her of stealing from the company. Kelly was appalled; the whole thing was obviously a big mistake. She tried to explain, but his mind was made up. Kelly was escorted off the property by a security guard.

Shocked, humiliated, angry, and frightened were just a few of the emotions Kelly felt as she drove down the interstate. She needed perspective and encouragement, but most of all she needed to let loose of her feelings. Pulling over on the shoulder, Kelly grabbed her cell phone, called one of her closest friends, and asked if she could borrow her for an hour. Together they drove a couple of blocks away to the site of an abandoned gravel pit. Kelly asked her friend to wait for her in the car for a few minutes.

Kelly walked several hundred feet and then started yelling. With fists clenched and tears flowing, she let it all out, venting her disappointment and anger to God. Finally, when she had spewed it all out, Kelly collapsed in a heap on the ground. Five minutes later a familiar hand touched her shoulder. "I'm here for you, too," her friend whispered.

When Kelly heard the gentleness and care in her friend's voice, she turned and saw that her friend had been crying...for her.

Kelly knows that God will always be there, but sometimes she needs friends as well.

We all need friends. We really do.

Something to Try

You can choose just one...

✳ Describe your best friend in grade school. What made her your best friend, and what are your favorite memories of her? If you know where she is, send her a letter or e-mail sharing these thoughts with her.

✳ What is the silliest thing you have ever done with a good friend? What is the most meaningful?

✳ If you are still developing a network of friends, look at the five ways to find a friend listed in the sidebar on page 131, and choose one idea that appeals to you. Determine to take the first step toward one of these activities sometime in the next ten days.

✳ You probably have a project you want to do (like painting a room or starting a garden) but just can't find the time. How about calling up a friend and offering to help her with one of her projects if she will help you with one of yours?

12

Burlap People

*Some people weave burlap into the fabric of our lives,
and some weave gold thread.
Both contribute to make the whole picture
beautiful and unique.*

AUTHOR UNKNOWN

I (Steve) wish I could join Will Rogers when he said, "I've never met a person I didn't like." But the truth is, I have. I've run into people who seem to have been put on this earth to irritate and stress me.

You've met them, too. You've encountered rude drivers and surly grocery store clerks. You've had demanding bosses who assign impossible or irrelevant tasks. You might struggle with relatives who are hurtful or deceitful or friends who are more frustrating than fun.

Difficult people are not necessarily bad; they just rub you the wrong way—and they can wear you out. They may push your buttons, belittle you, or set you on edge.

Years ago, Bob Dylan ended one of his songs with the idea that he wished a difficult person could be inside his shoes for just a single day—"then you'd know what a drag it is to see you." That's not exactly polite or socially appropriate, but if you're totally honest, you have to admit you've felt this way before. We all have difficult people in our lives with whom we must deal on a regular basis. The ones I hear the most complaints about are the following.

- *Controllers* insist on having everything their way. They are demanding and stubborn and rarely give in.

- *Clams* are quiet and withdrawn. It is hard to know what they want or like because they don't give you enough information.

- *Know-it-alls* are arrogant and condescending; they have this knack for making you feel stupid. They believe the world should and/or does revolve around them.

- *Complainers* always have something to grumble or gripe about. They seem to enjoy whining, but they rarely do anything to change the situation.

- *Bullies* are angry and sometimes abusive. They might be sarcastic, loud, pushy, threatening, or even physically abusive—anything to get their way.

- *Manipulators* are deceptive and indirect in making things happen. They take advantage of people to fulfill their own personal desires.

- *Addicts* are caught up in certain unhealthy patterns and are driven to do almost anything to meet their needs. They're willing to lie, cheat, and manipulate to get their next "fix."

- *Blockers* stand in the way of you and your goals. For reasons of jealousy, fear, or even misguided affection, they don't want you to move forward. They can be very nice on the surface, but their words and actions are calculated to discourage you and slow your progress.

Now admit it. You know people like this. They live in your neighborhood, go to your church, and work at your job. You might even be related or married to one. Sometimes they are actually *trying* to be difficult; often they don't have a clue they are such a problem. Either way, if you can develop some strategies for coping with difficult people, you can reduce your stress levels dramatically. Here are a few survival tips:

Burlap Survival Tip #1: Check Your Perception

One day when I was driving down the street, a car full of college guys started tailgating me. I sped up, but they kept right on my bumper, so close that they almost rear-ended me. As I got ticked at their recklessness, things got worse. They honked their horn, shook their fists at me, and shouted unintelligible words. I sped up more—five, ten, fifteen miles above the speed limit. They stayed right with me, but now they moved alongside my car and tried to force me off the road.

At this point I decided to confront these obnoxious punks. I pulled over to the side of the road and jumped out of the car.

"Didn't you see us?" one of the guys said as he ran up to me. "We've been trying to get your attention for the past ten miles. Something is wrong with your car. It's smoking and we were afraid it was going to start on fire or something."

It's amazing how fast my perspective changed. These obnoxious punks were now Good Samaritans.

The point is, it's easy to jump to the wrong conclusion. When your irritation level starts to rise because of a difficult person, it's always a good idea to make sure your perceptions are valid.

Burlap Survival Tip #2: Check Your Attitude

Sometimes your own stress might make you impatient, hypersensitive, and intolerant. A negative attitude might be the biggest factor in your problem, so an attitude check might be in order to make sure *you* aren't the difficult person in the situation. It's good to ask yourself, *Is the person really that difficult, or am I overreacting?*

Burlap Survival Tip #3: Accept Reality

"The most frustrating thing about teenagers is that they act so adolescent," an irate parent huffed to me. But that's just the way it is. Teenagers act adolescent. Obnoxious people act annoying. Debaters enjoy arguing. Certain people simply behave certain ways. You can cut your stress levels dramatically if you learn to acknowledge the inevitable. As you learn to recognize and expect these negative patterns, you won't be hit as hard emotionally.

Burlap Survival Tip #4: Look for the Lessons

Have you ever noticed that God seems to allow the same types of difficult people to enter your life over and over again? It's as if He is saying, "I want you to learn how to cope with this type of person."

Karen had an abusive father, has had numerous abusive boyfriends, and now has an abusive boss. With each of these people she tends to give away her power and does everything she can to gain their approval. The harder she tries, the more demanding they become. This sends her into a tailspin of self-deprecation and hopelessness. Until Karen learns that she doesn't have to tolerate abusive behavior and that there are some people she can't please, she will be trapped in what psychologists call a "repetition compulsion."

This is a common pattern for the worn-out woman—not necessarily the abuse, but the negative cycle of behavior and response. If you seem to be encountering the same kind of problem-people again and again, there might be something you need to learn. If you can learn to change your reaction or response—or just identify the pattern—you might avoid being pulled into other people's drama and dysfunction. With a little wisdom and insight you will know how to protect yourself from tears, sleepless nights, and moments when you think you're going crazy.

This is one of those situations, however, when the perspective of another person can help. A trusted, perceptive friend or a professional might be able to see your situation more objectively and help you think of ways to change your response.

Burlap Survival Tip #5: Try to Understand the Other Person

Difficult people are usually difficult for a reason. Taking the time to understand why they act the way they do might not motivate you to be closer to them, but it might help you be less angry or annoyed.

Everyone has a history, and this history helps explain why a person acts a certain way. A controller might feel out of control of her emotions, so she tries to overcontrol her environment. A clam might fear getting in trouble if he says anything, so he shuts up. A know-it-all might believe she is worthless if she doesn't have all the answers.

> It's a truth we want to pass on to our children:
> Nobody's perfect—
> we're all jerks saved by grace.
>
> KATHY PEEL

The world is full of broken people whose brokenness drives their behavior. The way they treat you often has very little to do with you; you just happen to be a convenient target. In fact, most difficult people have little or no insight into their own motives and behavior. Reminding yourself that there's a real, hurting person behind the challenging actions can sometimes turn your frustration into compassion.

You need to consider one more thing as you try to understand the difficult people in your life. There is always a chance that your weariness or past history is causing you to be a difficult person in someone else's life. The problem might be hers, but it might be yours as well. In any case, extending your understanding and compassion to yourself as well as others might significantly cut down on your people problems.

Burlap Survival Tip #6: Detach and Distance

The more time you spend with a difficult person, the more worn out and agitated you're likely to feel. You can counter this by learning to detach emotionally. Detaching means you distract yourself from thinking, worrying, or getting upset about this person. (One woman I heard about actually imagined herself inside a glass jar when she was with a difficult person—able to see and hear but unable to be touched or hurt.)

Detaching also involves listening to your own thoughts and clearing out any that empower your difficult people. Watch out for self-statements (or assumptions) like:

* I need her approval.
* I can't have him upset at me.
* I must agree with her.

❋ I can't allow her to hurt me.

❋ I must get him to understand.

❋ I have to do it her way.

Such thoughts not only indicate fear and anxiety; they also increase it. More important, they're lies. Letting them go unchallenged will only make the problem worse.

To emotionally detach, you might have to physically distance yourself—to decide calmly and rationally that it is not in your best interests to spend time around this person. This includes writing, e-mailing, phoning, talking with, or associating with the other person any more than absolutely necessary. There's no need to be mean about it; you don't have to be rude or gossip about the situation. You simply take control of your life and move on.

Obviously, in some situations, distancing yourself emotionally from another person might be problematic. If your difficult person happens to be your spouse, your children, or your parents, for instance, many other issues must be considered. In these special situations, it's best not to detach or distance yourself until you have thoroughly explored your options with a trained pastor, counselor, or psychologist.

Burlap Survival Tip #7: Defend Your Boundaries

Setting boundaries simply means that you determine your limits—what level of interaction you will permit with another person. A boundary is the place where the other person's rights end and yours begin. You may find it necessary to set physical boundaries ("I'm uncomfortable with you kissing and hugging me. I don't want you to do that anymore."), time boundaries ("I don't want to be called after nine unless it's a 911-level emergency."), or emotional boundaries ("I just can't be involved in your problems with your mother. When you bring this up again, I'm going to leave the room.").

Setting boundaries with other people can significantly lower your stress, but only if you are clear with yourself and others about what they are. This is not a time for hinting or subtlety; it's important that the other people get your message. You need to be direct and firm—as the apostle Paul reminds, to speak "the truth in love."[1]

Some Tips for Communicating Boundaries

- Stick to the main point.
- Keep it short.
- Leave the past in the past.
- Avoid arguing, blaming, or defending.
- Be positive.
- Watch your tone of voice.

It helps if a trusted friend or counselor can review your boundaries first to make sure you are being realistic and are accomplishing your goals without being hard-hearted. After that, the best approach is usually to go to the person and clearly tell him or her what your boundaries are (see the examples at the top of the previous page). If the process of being this direct is threatening and doesn't feel safe, take a good friend along as support. Her job is not to be a referee or to speak for you, but just to be there as a silent encourager. In certain cases you might choose to write out what you have to say and either mail it or hand it to the person.

Once you have set boundaries, it's important to enforce them. Be prepared to leave the room or confront the other person. If you find this process difficult—and many women do—don't hesitate to ask your friends or a counselor for support. You have the right to set limits on your interaction with other people.

Burlap Survival Tip #8:
Pray for the Other Person—and Yourself

Beloved pastor and bestselling author Ron Mehl was fond of saying, "Prayer is the first step to meeting any challenge." And difficult people obviously present a challenge. Jesus encourages us even more directly to "pray for those who persecute" us.[2]

Prayer can accomplish much more than we could ever imagine. It is the greatest tool any of us has when things go wrong. As theologian E. M. Bounds wrote, "Prayer is the possibility to affect everything that affects us." Clearly, difficult people fall in that category.

As you attempt to cope with the difficult people in your life, it's important to keep praying. Pray for their welfare and growth, and also pray about your attitude and actions toward them. Pray that you will show kindness and integrity regardless of what they do.

When you are already worn out, this may seem impossible. If you are feeling annoyed or irritated with another person, you might not even *want* to pray for him or her. But the Bible is clear that the Holy Spirit intercedes when we run up against our limits in prayer. All you really need to do is take the first step. Say the words, even if you don't feel them. Or tell God that you *want* to pray for the other person even if you are really mad at him or her. And then trust God to make your feeble prayers what they were meant to be.

151

It Takes All Kinds

There's probably no way to completely solve the problem of difficult people in your life. Someone will always rub you the wrong way—and you may rub others the wrong way as well. But how you respond to your people problems will make a big difference in how worn out you feel. The secret is to be polite and kind, but firm—showing respect but also asking respect from others. Sometimes, in the case of rude strangers, highway encounters, or annoying phone calls, the wisest course of action is to ignore it, walk away, and seek out more congenial company.

We can always hope that difficult people will change and become easier to be with. More likely, you will need to grow and learn how to cope with social challenges.

It helps to remember that as sinners we're all difficult people in our own ways. But God's love and grace have been extended to us all, and one of the requirements of following Him is that we extend that grace to others.

If you keep in mind that God loves even burlap people, you'll find it a lot easier to live past the itchy, scratchy irritation and keep your eyes on the beautiful fabric of your unfolding life.

Something to Try

You can choose just one...

※ Think of some of the burlap people in your life, and determine if they are really difficult or just in a difficult situation.

※ Consider what time and space you need to protect your sense of well-being. Write out some boundaries and review what you have written with a friend. If necessary, make a plan to present these boundaries to the person who needs to hear them.

※ Daily, for one week, commit to praying for one of the difficult people in your life.

※ It's time for a bubble bath. Load the tub with bubbles and scented oil. Grab a favorite magazine, and turn on some soothing music. Light a couple of candles, put a "Do Not Disturb" sign on the door, and relax. Just relax and enjoy—alone.

13

The Gift
of Forgiveness

*He who cannot forgive another
breaks the bridge over which he must pass himself.*

GEORGE HERBERT

t happens every September. Ten pounds of potatoes
are stuffed into brown gunnysacks and lined up at
the front of the classroom. The number of sacks
equals the number of freshmen students. The
teacher's challenge is simple: "This is an object lesson
about forgiveness. If you participate, you will learn one of
life's most valuable lessons.

"Select one of the bags and carry it with you everywhere. Tuck it into bed with you at night, drag it with you
on the bus, sling it over your shoulder when you're shopping. At the end of three weeks, dump the sack of potatoes
just outside the classroom door and give me a report."

Every year the students make three essential observations:

- The potatoes are heavy.
- They start to smell.
- It feels *great* to dump them!

That's also true of offenses—both what we have done and what others have done to us. In fact, the failure to deal with hurts is one of the primary reasons women feel exhausted and weary. Carrying a load of guilt or resentment takes a terrible toll—physically, emotionally, and spiritually. I read somewhere that 80 percent of health problems can be traced to the root cause of unforgivingness.

All this helps explain the results of a poll columnist Ann Landers took a number of years ago. She asked her readers to describe the best gift they had ever received. Letters poured in by the thousands. When all the responses were tallied up, the winner surprised everyone. For the vast majority of people, the best gift ever received was the gift of forgiveness.

When you think about it, it's easy to see why being forgiven can be a wonderful gift. It's really the gift of love and freedom, the gift of a second chance. But we sometimes forget that forgiveness can be as beneficial to the one giving it as it is to the one receiving it. Forgiveness, in other words, is not only a gift you give others; it is also a wonderful gift to give yourself.

Forgiveness is like resting your head on a pillow filled with rose petals instead of a pillow filled with thorns.

LOREN FISCHER

The trouble, of course, is that forgiveness can be costly. If your hurts are deep or recent, even reading this chapter may be difficult for you. But please don't skip over it. Instead, we suggest you ask the Holy Spirit to work on your heart as you read and to gently move you to the place where you might consider forgiveness.

It's possible you have carried pain for so long that you don't even notice how heavy the burden has become. Without your realizing it, these hurts are draining your energy and distracting you from a more fulfilling life. Once you take the steps to forgive someone who has caused you deep pain or even to forgive yourself for something you regret, you might be astonished at the fresh energy you have. Your outlook on life will improve and you'll wake up each day with new vitality.

The big question, of course, is *how* do you give the gift of forgiveness? A simple, glib "I forgive you" rarely cuts it. You might wish for a quick formula so you can check off each item and be done with it. But forgiveness is more a process than a once-and-for-all activity. As you move through the process step by step, you gradually begin to realize that something wonderful is taking place in your heart and setting you free. Here are seven steps that can help you find that freedom:

Forgiveness Step #1: Admit the Hurt and the Anger

It may sound strange, but the first step toward forgiving another person is to admit how hurt and angry you really are. Sometimes it seems easier just to pretend the hurt isn't important and try to forget about it. The trouble is, you don't forget. Offenses that wound your heart accumulate in your memory and keep you from experiencing the abundant life God has planned for you.

Walter Wangerin Jr. expresses it well: "When the heart is hurt, the eyes are blurred by tears, and the world itself is distorted."[1] The process of healing and forgiveness must begin with honesty. You don't want to minimize what happened, but you don't want to exaggerate it either. Truthfully look at what, if any, part you contributed to the problem. Writing down your memories and feelings about an event will help you determine if you are off balance. When you do this, try to step back and get some perspective as well as pouring out your feelings.

Forgiveness Step #2: Talk It Out

If you are in an ongoing relationship with someone who has hurt you, it is important that you talk about the hurt with the one who caused it. Try to choose a convenient time and a private place, but don't put off your conversation just because the circumstances aren't perfect. You will want to be open and honest while not slipping into an attack mode. Calmly express your perspective and feelings about what happened, and then invite the other person to do the same. Listen carefully, trying to understand without interrupting or becoming defensive. Remember that there are two sides to every story. Seeing the other side may not reduce the pain, but it may well soften your heart and help you forgive.

If a face-to-face meeting is not possible or advisable, you can still benefit from writing out the things you would otherwise say. Be specific about what the other person has done and how this has affected you. If appropriate, ask for clarification or state that you are in the process of trying to forgive. Whether or not you actually mail the letter, "talking it out" in this way will move you one more step down the road to forgiveness.

How to Talk It Out (with Someone Who Has Hurt You)

- ✳ Share your hurt and let the other person see your heart.
- ✳ With a calm voice, explain how the offense has affected you.
- ✳ Don't accuse, attack, insult, belittle, or use sarcasm.
- ✳ Use positive statements wherever you can.
- ✳ Use "I" statements like "I feel hurt because..."
- ✳ Avoid "you" statements like "You are the one who..."
- ✳ Stay on the subject.
- ✳ Maintain eye contact.
- ✳ Try to *talk* about your anger without acting it out.
- ✳ Listen to the other person's viewpoint.
- ✳ Don't interrupt.
- ✳ Speak as though God is listening. (He is.)

Forgiveness Step #3:
Remember Why Forgiveness Is Necessary

"Be kind to one another, tender-hearted, forgiving each other, *just as God in Christ also has forgiven you.*"[2] The last part of this verse is a great reminder of *why* you need to forgive others.

The truth is, we all carry the weight of the careless, hurtful, or terribly wrong things we have done, and we all have abundant need of forgiveness. The amazing thing is that when we come to God, confess our sin, and ask forgiveness...He forgives us. The Bible says it clearly: "If we confess our sins to him, he is faithful and just to forgive us and to cleanse us from every wrong."[3]

Jesus has already died to pay the price for your mistakes, and He longs for you to accept His free gift of forgiveness. But He wants something else, too. He wants you to forgive others—not necessarily because they deserve it, not even because forgiving is good for you, but because He forgave you first.

Accepting God's forgiveness and forgiving others are like two sides of the same coin. They're both necessary if you want to be the person God has in mind for you to be—and avoid lugging around all that guilt and resentment. Besides, if Christ has given you the gift of forgiveness, how can you refuse to offer it to others?

Forgiveness Step #4: Choose Forgiveness

Forgiveness essentially means giving up your right to make other people pay for the wrongs they have committed against you. It's a choice, a decision of the will. And it's good to keep in mind that the choice of forgiveness almost always precedes the *feeling* of forgiveness. When you first make the choice to forgive, you might still feel angry or resentful. By choosing forgiveness, you are asking God to take your willingness and gradually work a miracle in your heart. But it may take time—not because forgiveness doesn't work, but because your emotional wounds still need time to heal.

Forgiveness Step #5: Put the Hurt Behind You

The mind is a fabulous computer that usually runs seventy years or more without warranty work. I read somewhere that it can record up to eight hundred memories per second, storing the more significant memories for a lifetime. (Don't you wonder how scientists determine that?) This means that the old saying "forgive and forget" really isn't very likely. But since forgetting is not really a prerequisite for healing a hurt, it's not a necessary part of forgiveness. What is necessary is making a decision to stop rehearsing the pain over and over. Once we have faced what has happened to us, we can be done with reliving the past and rehashing the details. Memories will rise in our mind, but we can choose to put them away and focus on other things.

According to Ken Sande, author of *The Peacemaker*, putting hurts behind us involves making four promises:

* I will no longer dwell on this incident.
* I will not bring up this incident again and use it against you.
* I will not talk to others about this incident.
* I will not allow this incident to stand between us or hinder our relationship.[4]

Forgiveness Step #6: Be Patient with the Process

It would be nice if the process of forgiveness happened quickly, but often it doesn't. Some hurts are just too painful to let go of, even when we truly *want* to forgive. It takes time to put the pain behind us and move forward. But as the days pass, we usually come to realize that forgiveness has taken hold in our hearts and we are beginning to trust again.

This process is complicated when the other person hurts us again, as is almost inevitable in a very close relationship such as a marriage. In this cycle of hurt, forgiveness, and trust, the forgiveness must be repeated over and over.

In cases of abuse, renewed trust may be inappropriate or even unsafe, and it is vitally important to seek help from a pastor or trained professional. But usually the cycle is part of the ordinary struggles that deepen our commitment to one another as we work through them. When relationships are restored through the process of giving and receiving forgiveness, they can even become more durable. Like a treasured porcelain vase that has been accidentally broken but is too precious to discard, we lovingly mend the vessel. Sometimes the glue makes it stronger.

Forgiveness Step #7: Forgive Yourself

It is not enough to forgive others. We must also learn to forgive ourselves—and to accept the gift of God's forgiveness. This is often the most difficult step because we feel that the guilt-producing secrets we carry in our heart are too horrible for forgiveness. Remember that God is willing to forgive everything and, indeed, has already forgiven if you have asked Him to. He wants you to move forward and stop punishing yourself.

If you are struggling with ongoing guilt issues in your life, try adapting the steps of the forgiveness process and applying them to your own heart. *Admit* that you have failed. *Talk it out* with God and others you have disappointed or hurt. *Remember* God's forgiveness. *Choose forgiveness* by accepting what God has offered. *Try to put the pain behind you* and look forward. And *be patient with the process* of coming to terms with the beautiful reality of God's forgiveness.

In his classic booklet *My Heart—Christ's Home*, Robert Boyd Munger uses the example of a house to describe how "room by room" we turn our hearts over to Christ. For example, he talks about the Living Room, where we develop intimacy through prayer and reading the Bible, and the Library, which holds things that occupy our minds. But the last room Munger describes is the Hall Closet—the place where we keep the secret things of our heart. And it is in this place that we find the key to forgiving others and ourselves:

> One day I found Christ waiting for me at the door. An arresting look was in His eye. As I entered He said to me, "There is a peculiar odor in the house. Something must be dead around here. It's upstairs. I think it is in the hall closet." As soon as He said this, I knew what He was talking about....
>
> With trembling fingers I passed the key to Him. He took it, walked over to the door, opened it, entered, took out all the putrefying stuff that was rotting there, and threw it away. Then He cleaned the closet and painted it. It was done in a moment's time. Oh, what victory and release to have that dead thing out of my life.[5]

For every person—for every worn-out woman—the glorious gifts of forgiveness are victory and release. They are gifts that make your heart sing.

Something to Try

You can choose just one...

✳ Look up these verses in your Bible and carefully
consider how wonderful they are. Put a heart by
each verse...or at least by your favorites.

1 John 1:9	Ephesians 2:8–9
Psalm 103:12	1 Timothy 1:15
Psalm 51:7	Romans 8:38–39

✳ What hurts, offenses, or regrets are you having a
hard time letting go of? How is this affecting the way
you feel about yourself, about others, about life in
general, and about God?

✳ Review Ken Sande's four promises of letting go. Which
ones are easiest for you? Which ones are hardest?

✳ Many of us have areas of our life where we feel we
are not worthy of God's forgiveness. On a blank piece
of paper, write one that you struggle with. Next, in
bold letters across the page, write, "Forgiven forever!"
Then take the paper and shred it, burn it, or bury it.

Worry Is a Rocking Chair

Worry is like a rocking chair.
It will give you something to do,
but it won't get you anywhere.

Worry is an incredible drain for worn-out women. Yet so many women just can't seem to stop worrying about their families, their jobs, their relationships, and their finances. No matter what our circumstances, most of us can usually find something to worry about.

Worry is not the same thing as being concerned about problems. We all have difficulties, and it's appropriate to be concerned enough to want to solve them. If we weren't concerned, we might never do anything to improve our lives.

But worry, by definition, never improves anything. Worry is that continual rehearsal of what has gone wrong in your life or what *might* go wrong. It's stewing over what you can't change or regretting what you did or didn't do. Like a dog with a bone, you just keep gnawing on whatever makes you anxious. And that is harmful because:

✳ *Worry feeds on itself.* The more you worry, the more you can usually find to worry about.

✳ *Worry gets you stuck* emotionally, mentally, spiritually, and physically. Instead of taking steps to move forward, you get caught in a cycle of *but*s and *what if*s.

✳ *Worry steals your joy* because it undermines your trust in God and distances you from Him.

✳ *Worry hurts your relationships,* especially if it pushes you to nag or complain.

✳ *Worry drains your energy.* It either speeds you up—pushing you to do more and more to head off frightening possibilities. Or it can shut you down, paralyzing you with fear and anxiety. Either way it siphons off energy you could be using to solve your problems.

✳ *Worry robs you of peace.* How can you feel peaceful or serene when your mind is full of anxiety?

✳ *Worry can actually make you sick.* Chronic anxiety and worry have been linked to weakened immune systems, cardiovascular disease, neurological imbalance, and clinical depression, not to mention specific anxiety-related illnesses such as panic attacks.

What's Your Worry Style?

One of the interesting things about worry is that every person seems to handle it differently. Some people deliberately cultivate a "What? Me worry?" attitude by refusing to face what is really bothering them. Others seem to soak up worries even when they try not to. Then there are those who tend to "catastrophize"—a small worry triggers another, then another, until the issue seems unsolvable and the whole world looks dark and gloomy.

Some people are nighttime worriers. They're fine during the day, but when things slow down, usually late at night, those worries creep in and take over. Some people keep their worry inside, building up tension and feeding their ulcers. Others inflict their worry on others with chronic complaining, outbursts of anger, constant nagging, or using their worry to instill guilt. Some even use worry as a source of pride, fooling themselves into thinking they only worry because they "care so much."

Whatever the style, worry does more damage than most people realize. In *How to Stop Worrying and Start Living*," Dale Carnegie tells a story about a gigantic tree that lies fallen on a mountain slope in Colorado. The tree was a seedling when Columbus came to America and was half grown when the Pilgrims landed at Plymouth Rock. During the course of its long life, it was struck by lightning fourteen times, stood against many avalanches, and weathered innumerable storms. The tree survived all these onslaughts. However, in the end, an army of beetles attacked it. These small insects ate their way through the bark and slowly, bite by bite, destroyed the heart of the tree. Soon this giant tree crashed to the forest floor.[1]

Worry can be like that. Little by little, it can send all your dreams and possibilities crashing to the ground.

But God wants so much more for you. Whatever your

style of worry, God wants you to give it up. He wants you to give Him all your worries and let Him work things out according to His good and loving will.

Jesus said it plainly and directly: "Don't worry."[2] In the Sermon on the Mount, He said it at least three times. This "isn't a suggestion," as Joanna Weaver beautifully points out. "It's a command. Worry and/or anxiety is specifically mentioned twenty-five times in the New Testament alone as something we should avoid."[3]

If you're a chronic worrier, that may be easier said than done. Worry is a habit that can be tricky to break. Here are a few ideas that can help you short-circuit worry and substitute peace and contentment.

Worry Buster #1: Try to Calm Down

When you realize you have begun to fall into that familiar pattern of worry, the first thing to do is to try to calm yourself down. Take a deep breath, then another. Gently stretch the muscles in your hands, your neck, and your shoulders, which are probably tense and tight. Walk around, shake out your hands, and take some more deep breaths. If you have a Bible nearby, read through Matthew 6:25–34 or a favorite passage that usually calms your heart. You might even ask yourself what my grandmother used to ask me as a small child: "What difference will this make a year from now?"

Worry Buster #2: Sort Out Your Concerns

Remember the Serenity Prayer? One of the reasons that little prayer by Reinhold Niebuhr is quoted so often is that it helps us remember that there are situations we can fix and others we must simply live with, asking God for the grace not to crumple. Worry doesn't help in either case. But figuring out which is which can assist you in sorting out the issues that cause you worry.

> *God, grant me the serenity to accept the things I cannot change;*
> *courage to change the things I can;*
> *and the wisdom to know the difference.*
> *Living one day at a time;*
> *enjoying one moment at a time;*
> *accepting hardship as the pathway to peace;*
> *taking, as He did, this sinful world as it is, not as I would have it;*
> *trusting that He will make all things right, if I surrender to His will;*
> *that I may be reasonably happy in this life,*
> *and supremely happy with Him forever in the next. Amen.*
>
> REINHOLD NIEBUHR[4]

When worry begins to knot your stomach, stop and take a good look at what is worrying you. It helps to actually write out your worries so you can see them in black and white. We also encourage you to talk them out with a trusted friend. Look for exaggeration that has increased your worry. Then ask yourself, "Is this something I actually have control over? Is there anything I can do about this problem right now or in the near future?"

Worry Buster #3: Take Action If You Can

Writer and speaker Donna Otto is fond of saying that it's not the things we do that cause us stress; it's the things we *don't* do.[5] You can cut down on a lot of worry if you actually take steps to address whatever is bothering you. Even if you can't immediately solve a problem, you can probably outline the issues, ask advice, develop a plan, or gather information so you can better understand what you're worrying about. If your feelings of anxiety are severe and overwhelming, it's important to see a physician or counselor to help you seek out and resolve the root causes before they build into something more serious.

What if you find you really can't do anything about an issue that is worrying you? What if it is simply out of your control? Some things you must place in God's hands, knowing that He is Master of all.

Worry Buster #4: Turn Your Worries Over to the Lord

"Give all your worries and cares to God," the apostle Peter reminds us, "for he cares about what happens to you."[6] That, in the end, is the only truly effective response to worry. Instead of gnawing at that bone of worry, you need to deliberately and consistently turn your anxieties over to

Him and trust Him to work everything out.

When you trust God, the apostle Paul tells us, "you will experience God's peace, which is far more wonderful than the human mind can understand."[7] The opposite of worry is peace. In the same verse, Paul goes on to say that God's peace can "guard your heart and mind." What a great promise in an age of anxiety!

Worry Buster #5: When Worries Return, Distract Yourself

Even when you resolve to give all your worries to the Lord, worry can be a persistent habit. Whenever it starts to nag at you, it's important to short-circuit that process. Whatever you can do to distract yourself from your worrisome thoughts will help. If you're lying in bed worrying, get up, walk around, perhaps read a book—or pull out your journal and write down what has been bothering you. If you've fallen into daydreaming about your worries, get up and stretch, take a walk, or play with the dog. Some people even keep a rubber band around their wrist and gently snap it to remind themselves to "snap out of" their worry.

Worry does not empty tomorrow of its sorrow;
it empties today of its strength.

CORRIE TEN BOOM

Once you've successfully distracted yourself, try to refocus on something else—something positive and encouraging.

Spending time in Scripture can be an especially effective worry antidote because it reminds you again and again of God's power and the importance of trust. Conversation is also a helpful way to both distract yourself and refocus your attention. That's because interaction with other people pulls you out of your own internal world, where worry and anxiety tend to grow. By keeping you in the present, at least momentarily, social interaction can chase away all worries about the past and the future.

Some people also find it helpful to consciously postpone their stubborn worry, setting aside a specific "worry time" each day. They actually set a timer for ten minutes and spend that time focusing on all the *what if*s that tend to occupy their minds. When the timer rings and "worry time" is over, they set their worries aside, knowing they'll have a chance to revisit them later. By learning to postpone worry, they're actually taking steps toward giving it up altogether.

174

Worry Buster #6: Build Your Trust Muscles

Ultimately, learning to trust God is the answer to any problem. But worry tends to be a stubborn pattern, so replacing it with a habit of trust takes time. It's a process of facing each concern, doing what you can, and then handing it over to God—resisting the temptation to snatch it back. Some people find it helps to actually visualize the process of placing those squirming little worries into the Father's strong and capable hands.

The good news is that the more worries you give over to the Father, the more your trust tends to grow. You'll enjoy moving forward instead of wasting your energy on the rocking chair of worry. You'll grow closer to the Lord, understanding at a personal level that He is good enough and loving enough to take care of anything you hand Him—even your most excruciating concerns.

Life Outside the Rocking Chair

I (Steve) will never forget Patricia, a twenty-seven-year-old mother of two with a devoted husband, a great job, and a beautiful home. She also had an ulcer, hadn't had a good night's sleep in almost six months, and rarely smiled. She worried about everything, and the more she worried, the worse her life seemed to become.

One night, Patricia's heart started pounding so hard it felt as if it would explode. She could barely catch her breath and felt like the room was spinning. Her husband called 911 and an ambulance rushed her to the hospital, where the doctor told them her symptoms were caused by anxiety.

The next day Patricia pleaded with God to show her how to let go of her worries. With the help of her family and a counselor, she began choosing to trust God one step at a time. Although it wasn't easy and things didn't change quickly, now Patricia feels like a new person. She still has her worn-out moments, but life is definitely better.

You can tell by her radiant smile.

Something to Try

You can choose just one...

※ What sort of things did your family worry about when you were a child? What were your mother's biggest concerns? Do you also carry some of these worries or cares?

※ Read and meditate on Matthew 6:25–34, which is Jesus' longest sermon on worry. If you wish, paraphrase the passage to apply more specifically to your life.

※ Search for an activity that gets your mind off your worries. Consider anything from exercise to reading to gardening to calling a good friend. Look at your schedule and consider how you might make this activity part of your daily routine.

※ Every home should have a kite! See if you can find a wonderful, brightly colored kite that flies well. Enjoy getting it all assembled; then leave it out in plain sight as a reminder. Watch for a day with a playful breeze and rush outdoors and let both your kite and your spirits soar.

15

When Dreams Shatter

I have a God who hears me,
I have a God who's near.
I have a God who's waiting
with a bottle for my tears.

KIMBER ANNE ENGSTROM

a s soon as I (Alice) answered the phone, I knew something was wrong. My friend Jan's voice was barely recognizable. After her choked hello there was a long pause before she could continue.

Jan's husband had come home early from work that day, while the children were still at school, and told her he was moving out. He had been seeing someone else for a long time, he said, and although he still loved her, he just didn't want to live at home anymore. Jan begged and pleaded, but he packed a few belongings and left. All her hopes and dreams for a successful marriage left with him. She had spent more than two hours crumpled in a corner sobbing before she was able to call me.

It seems this was a week for broken dreams. Our friend Judy, a wonderful single mom, discovered drugs in her son's room. This was the same son who had been voted most valuable player on his basketball team just a few weeks earlier. She had felt so proud at the banquet watching her tall, handsome sixteen-year-old receive his trophy. Now Judy's disappointment was so powerful that she could barely get out of bed in the mornings.

What do you do when your joy is replaced by sorrow? When dreams shatter and you're left with a broken heart? When you find yourself wondering if God hears your prayers or even cares about your struggles?

When life takes a terrible turn, we want to remind you that after the tears of nighttime, joy really does come in the morning.[1] If tears have come to live in your heart, it is likely they have brought companions of fatigue and heaviness. But joy will return, and she will bring vitality and life. If you are worn out because of disappointments, we pray that this chapter will help you keep going through the night, waiting expectantly for the dawn of joy.

Sometimes I get worn out just thinking about the heartaches my friends are facing, and then when discouraging personal news plunges *me* into darkness, I'm slow at coping. I'm even slower when I try to blame God for my disappointments. I don't want to hear about His love, His power, or His perfect timing. Even though the wounded place in my heart longs for His comfort, my first reaction is to withdraw into a gloomy mood with a heavy gray blanket wrapped around my spirit. I sob and groan and yell angry words until all that remains of my tears is a silent dampness on flushed cheeks.

Sometimes it's hours, sometimes weeks, before I

notice—but I'm not alone in my gloomy place. God is there with me. He holds a glistening bottle in His hands where He has gathered my tears as though they were precious.[2] The awareness of His tender lovingkindness begins to lift the gray blanket, and I'm ready to press close to Him, waiting for the joy to finally dawn.

Desperate sorrows as well as an accumulation of ordinary disappointments can wear all of us down and wear us out. They can prevent us from enjoying the pleasant aspects of life and rob us of our confidence in God.

In a way, of course, we set ourselves up for disappointment because we cling to false expectations. We know better, but part of us still insists that life should always turn out right—constant good health, children never becoming prodigals, cheaters never prospering, no personal regrets over choices made. Then, when night falls and our dreams come crashing down around us, we question God, who never promised that everything would be great. What He promised was to always be with us—and He always keeps that promise.

Like me, many of you have a heart to press closer to God, not to push away. You want to let go of the feeling of weariness and grab hold of joy again. I'd like to share six things that have helped me. I use the acronym *CLOSER* because it helps me remember them: Come. Lean. Open. Surrender. Eternalize. Release.

How to Draw C-L-O-S-E-R to God

Come to Him

Lean on Him

Open your Bible

Surrender your expectations

Eternalize your thoughts

Release everything to God

C—Come

Jesus constantly invited people to come and spend time with Him. Can you imagine how thrilled you would be if you received a personal invitation to talk over your concerns with the president of the United States, the queen of England, or some other head of state? And here you have the King of kings, the Lord of lords, the One whose name is above every other name, inviting you to spend time with Him. He wants to listen, to comfort, to help. Let His words connect with your longings: "Come to me, all of you who are weary and carry heavy burdens, and I will give you rest."[3]

When you come to Him, you are beginning to press closer.

L—Lean

Who do you lean on when things upset you? The answer will make a big difference in how worn out you feel.

Even though my mother paid her rent in life's heartbreak hotel, she exhibited steady peace, grace, and vitality. She looked for opportunities to use her experiences to give God-centered hope to others. When she was going through an especially difficult time, I remember her saying, "I don't know where my Good Shepherd is taking me, but I'll keep leaning on Him all the way."

The Lord is good for leaning. He is strong and steady. He will never leave you or forsake you. He has called you by name and made you His. When you pass through the deep waters, He has promised to be with you.[4]

When you are leaning on Him, you are pressing closer.

> *When you are leaning on Him, you are pressing closer.*
> *The weaker we feel, the harder we lean on God.*
> *And the harder we lean, the stronger we grow.*
>
> JONI EARECKSON TADA

O—Open Your Bible

God wants his Word to be an oasis for your soul. He has filled it with comfort verses that fit your heartbreak.

The Psalms, especially, speak directly to our disappointments with words of comfort. Read Psalm 23 for a lovely picture of God's personal care. Browse through Psalm 30 for a heartfelt commiseration and a gentle reminder that hope in God is never misplaced. Psalms 42, 46, 57, and 91 have carried many people through the dark night of their disappointment.

But the Psalms are not the only source of biblical comfort. Your own Bible is probably already marked with verses that are precious to you.[5] Use them freely as sources of comfort—that's part of why the Lord gave us the Bible in the first place. Use bookmarks and a highlighter to flag them for easy reference. (I like to write notes in the margin.) Read these special passages aloud as prayers. You might even try inserting your name to help you realize that God is talking to you through the Scriptures.

When you open God's love letter, you are pressing closer.

S—Surrender

I sometimes doubt God because I don't think He is working things out *my* way or on *my* time schedule. (How's that for pride and control issues!) Surrendering means trusting *God's* way and *God's* time schedule.

I like what Oswald Chambers said about this: "Your heavenly Father will explain it all one day. He cannot just yet because He is developing your character. 'Forget the character,' you say. 'I want Him to grant my request now.' And He says, 'What I am doing far exceeds what you can see or know. Trust Me.'"

When you surrender, you are pressing closer.

E—Eternalize

I remember times when I would discuss my disappointments with Pastor Loren Fischer. He would remove his glasses and lay them down on his desk and say, "We are seeing this through our viewpoint." Then, as he opened the Bible, he would deliberately pick up his glasses and while putting them on say, "Let's try and find God's perspective."

What Have You Lost?

A man once went to a minister for counseling.
He was in the midst of a financial collapse.
"I've lost everything," he bemoaned.
"Oh, I'm sorry to hear that you've lost your faith."
"No," the man corrected him, "I haven't lost my faith."
"Well, then I'm sad to hear that you've lost your character."
"I didn't say that," he corrected. "I still have my character."
"I'm so sorry to hear that you've lost your salvation."
"That's not what I said," the man objected.
"I haven't lost my salvation."
"You have your faith, your character, your salvation.
Seems to me," the minister observed, "that you've
lost none of the things that really matter."

MAX LUCADO[9]

Oh, what comfort to cling to what we know as absolute truth. There is a God and He loves us. Even when life is not always fair, God is. Even better, He's merciful! One day He will return and make all the wrongs right.

When you are looking at things through an eternal perspective, it's easier to press closer.

R—Release

Release means giving everything to God. It means packing up all the worry, all the *what ifs*, all the doubts, all the debris from our shattered dreams, and giving them to Him.

I still struggle with this. I throw it all in a mental suitcase and carry it to God. Then, after unpacking everything, item by item in prayer, I tend to throw most of it back in the suitcase and keep lugging it around instead of leaving it all with Him. And all the time wondering why I am so worn out!

Barbara Johnson is a gifted speaker and writer who uses her infectious humor and deep faith to encourage others—her writing has helped me a lot with this issue. In her book *Fresh Elastic for Stretched Out Moms,* she talks about letting go and letting God take your problems. She suggests picturing in your mind that you are placing whatever breaks your heart into a gift box wrapped with lovely paper and ribbon. Then imagine walking into a glorious throne room where Jesus is waiting. Place the package at His feet and wait as He bends down and lovingly picks it up. After He removes the wrapping, He tenderly holds the gift close in His arms.[6]

What a comforting image—Jesus holding our problems in His strong and caring arms. It's okay to look back now and then to reassure yourself that Jesus still holds your sorrow close to His heart.

When you release your gift of sorrow and disappointment to Him, you have pressed closer.

We will always want to have someone cherish us, to escape illness, to enjoy financial freedom, to see our plans succeed, to have our loved ones live in ways that please God. But hurts and disappointments will keep happening. It's part of the journey of life.

When dreams shatter and joy disappears...when night falls and the tears won't stop...try pressing closer to the Lord. Not only will He comfort you; He'll also give you a crown of beauty for your ashes. He will give you oil of gladness for your mourning. He will give you a garment of praise for your spirit of despair.[7]

And when morning comes to bring you joy, He'll still be there, holding you close to His heart.

Something to Try

You can choose just one...

* Recall what someone said or did to comfort you when you were hurting. What did it feel like, and how did it nurture your soul?

* Write out one or two verses from the comfort Psalms listed in this chapter (on page 181)—or use some of your own favorite verses. Place your name within the text to help you remember just how personal God's offer of comfort is.

* Review Barbara Johnson's gift package illustration, and give all your brokenness to Him. Try it right now before anything distracts you.

* Here's any easy yet elegant gift to make for yourself, and it only takes a couple of minutes. Find a pretty ribbon that's at least an inch wide (velvet and tapestry styles are nice). Trim the top with pinking shears so it won't ravel. Fold up the other end to a point and tack it with a couple of stitches. Sew a bead or charm onto the end of the point to weight the bookmark and add a pretty touch.[8]

16

Starting Your Day Right

I have always felt that the moment
when first you wake up in the morning
is the most wonderful of the twenty-four hours.
No matter how weary or dreary you may feel,
you possess the certainty that...
absolutely anything may happen.

MONICA BALDWIN

What's morning like at your house? If you're like many women, you start your day with a loud alarm and a buzz of hectic activity. You mainline caffeine, dig for something clean to wear, nag your kids to get ready, and remind your husband of something he needs to do that day. Are family squabbles part of your morning ritual? Does the TV or radio blare? Or are you so comatose in the mornings that you find yourself at your first appointment of the day without being quite sure how you managed to get there?

What happens in the morning is important, because how you start off each morning sets the stage for the rest of your day. It positions your energy, your mood, and your attitude for all that is to follow. If your morning does not begin well, the rest of the day becomes a little more difficult. But a well-orchestrated morning can set up a positive melody that carries you through the most challenging and draining of days.

How different people handle mornings is partly a matter of individual body rhythm. Some people naturally wake up with more energy than others. But almost anyone can make her mornings—and her life—go better by understanding and applying seven simple suggestions.

Establish a Positive Routine

Routines can relieve a lot of stress by removing the need to make decisions or solve problems when you might not be fully awake. If you are not a morning person, you may find it especially helpful to set up routines that take you through the first half-hour of the day more or less on autopilot. But even if you're the type to wake up fully alert and ready to tackle the morning, a healthful routine can be a source of comfort, freedom, and even extra energy for the day ahead.

Chances are, of course, that you already have a routine of sorts. The question is, is it a healthy, helpful routine? If every morning consists of staggering out of bed into the shower, gulping a cup or two of coffee while you listen to the news and supervise breakfast, running a load of laundry, then throwing on your clothes and putting on your makeup in the car, you may be digging your worn-out rut a little deeper every morning.

If mornings are a source of stress for you, we suggest you take a minute to examine your morning routine (or lack of it). What could you do to reduce your stress levels and start your mornings in a more positive light? Making even one positive change in your morning routine can make a dramatic difference.

Begin Your Morning the Night Before

One of the most helpful routines you can develop is to begin preparing for morning the night before. Whatever you do before you go to bed is one less thing to remember in the morning.

189

If you are a night person who needs at least a half hour after rolling out of bed to get your mind and body warmed up, preparing the night before is especially important. But even morning people can benefit from advance preparation. Here are some things you can do:

* *Decide what you will wear* ahead of time, check if everything's clean, and set out your clothes and accessories.

* *Set your clock radio* to wake you in the most positive way possible. Many people find music less jarring than a harsh, annoying buzzer. You can even buy alarm clocks that wake you by gradually increasing the light in the room. Think ahead to what you want

to do when you get up, and allow enough time to do it without panic. A peaceful morning is worth thirty minutes less sleep.

✳ *Set your automatic coffeemaker* to start a half hour before you have to get up. You might even want to set the table for breakfast.

✳ *Set your mind to get to bed* and turn off the lights at a consistent time that is early enough to give you a healthy amount of sleep.

If you are so worn out that you tend to fall asleep before you can even begin these nighttime preparations, try doing them right after dinner. Make them part of your after-dinner cleanup routine—wash the dishes, put them away, then get out tomorrow's clothes and set the alarm. Then you won't have to remember later, and you'll still have a head start on your day.

190

Each day comes bearing its own gifts.
Untie the ribbons.

RUTH ANN SCHABACKER

Ease Yourself into the Day

C. S. Lewis wrote: "The very moment you wake up each morning...all your wishes and hopes for the day rush at you like wild animals. And the first job each morning consists simply in shoving them all back; in listening to that other voice, taking that other point of view, letting that other, larger, stronger, quieter life come flowing in."[1]

If you can learn to do this—consciously placing your day in God's hands before you even try to greet the world—you'll have a daily head start.

Instead of giving in to the noise, the hectic activity, and the dread that sometimes pulls at you even before you step from your bed, take a moment to allow the "peace that passes all understanding" to surround you and fill you. This reminds you of who is in control—that there is a purpose and pattern in the most difficult, perplexing, and unfair of situations. When you know you are in the hollow of the Lord's hand, everything seems all right, and even in the darkest morning you are confident the sun has risen.

With this in mind, we suggest setting your alarm a little earlier than usual so you can ease into the day. If you can wake up to music, let your clock radio gently wake you up, and keep the music on long enough to set a positive attitude for your morning. Before you get out of bed, stretch and breathe deeply to wake up your body. To wake up your spirit, thank God for three blessings in your life. To wake up your mind and point it in a positive direction, try to think of two things you are looking forward to during the day.

One young lady I (Steve) know took this idea of easing into the day even further. She was determined to start right, so she bought her favorite chocolate truffles. Each night before she went to bed, she would set her treat on the night-stand and whisper, "See you tomorrow." The first thing she did the next morning was eat her truffle. She told me that was her way of making sure each morning was sweet.

Energize Your Body

Your body is programmed to respond to light, so you'll probably awake more easily if you open the curtains and pull up the blinds. If it's still dark or gray outside, turn on the lights—a lot of lights. (If you share a bedroom with someone who sleeps later than you do, of course you'll have to go into another room in order to do this.)

If you need caffeine to get going in the morning, fill a special cup and savor the taste. If you want to start a really healthy habit, however, drink a glass of water first thing to replenish fluids lost during the night. Then put on an upbeat, bouncy, energetic CD—something you love. To get your blood flowing faster, do a few more stretches and then a little aerobic exercise—dance, jump, jog in place, anything that gets your body moving. Even five minutes of movement will help start your day on a more energetic note.

Whether you choose to do a more serious workout in the morning depends on your schedule and your body clock. Many people find that early-morning exercise—a jog or fast walk, a few laps in the pool, or even an "early bird" class at the gym—wakes them up, stimulates their metabolism, and lessens the chance that they will skip exercise altogether. Some have told me that they're more likely to exercise if they get themselves going before they have a chance to really wake up and realize what they're doing!

Eat Your Best Meal

You've heard it before: "Breakfast is the most important meal of the day." That's especially true if you're a worn-out woman. Your body has been without food during the night and needs fuel to get you through your busy day.

You'll get an extra energy boost if you make this meal simple but special—a feast for the body and the spirit. If you can, eat it in your favorite room, using your favorite dishes. At the very least, sit down instead of just standing at the kitchen counter. Pour a glass of the most delicious fruit juice and sip it like it's the finest champagne, enjoying the fragrance and bright color. Look for ways to include protein to balance your blood sugar levels and carry you through the morning on a more even keel—maybe a spoonful of peanut butter or a few dry-roasted almonds. Relish fresh foods whenever possible.

Give Your Senses a Treat

Enjoying your breakfast is just one way to brighten your day by treating your senses to a dose of beauty. If you shower in the morning, use a scented shampoo and body wash. Invest in a showerhead that gives you just the right spray and pressure; then enjoy the feel of the water as it hits you. (You might even want to sing as you shower.) If you have to shower anyway, why not make it a source of pleasure?

Whatever else you do, set aside a moment to open your window or step out on your porch to get a sense of the weather and enjoy the season. Take a minute to soak in the beauty of God's creation—to really open up your senses. Reminding yourself of the incredible world around you can set a tone of gratitude and peace for the entire day.

Glory in the Morning

It's 5:30 A.M., and Day knocks at the dark doors of Night.
I sit on my porch swing under a dark green umbrella
of maple leaves that hover maternally over the porch roof.
And I wait for Sun....
Curtains of Night draw back silently,
and Sun bursts merrily over the blue haze of distant hills,
painting earth in green and brown stripes.
It is morning...and it is glorious!

LINDA ANDERSEN[2]

Give Yourself a Boost

Even on the most hectic morning, you could probably use an extra boost to improve your attitude, increase your energy, and give your day a positive start. Here are a few ideas that take hardly any time at all. Try to fit in at least one or two—or come up with your own ideas:

※ Read a one-page devotion.

※ Turn the page on an inspirational flip calendar and really think about the day's entry.

※ Reread a favorite poem.

※ Ask one of your kids to tell you a joke.

※ Write down three things you like about yourself.

※ Give your husband an extra long good-bye kiss.

※ Take five minutes to play with your dog or cat.

※ Pull out a sweet card or note from someone you care about, and read it through again.

※ Read your favorite comics in the paper.

※ Take five minutes to write a quick thank-you note or card you've been meaning to write. Put it in the mailbox.

195

No matter what else you choose to do—even if you choose to have your "quiet time" later in the day—take a moment for a quick prayer before your day begins. Give the day to the Lord. Thank Him for His blessings. Ask Him to show you His will for that day and to protect you.

A Strategy for Framing Your Day

It's possible you are looking back at the suggestions in this chapter and throwing your hands up—or snickering. Such a peaceful, energy-producing morning routine may simply seem out of reach. But we encourage you to try at least a few of the suggestions in this chapter—and see what a difference those few minutes can make.

It might help to think of your day as a jigsaw puzzle—lots of pieces, lots of shapes, lots of colors. Each morning you spread out pieces, and the task can look pretty overwhelming. But if you develop a strategy, things will start coming together. Developing a useful and positive morning routine is a bit like putting together the straight-edged pieces to make a frame around a puzzle. Once you do that, the other pieces quickly find their places.

Start your morning right, and you'll have the best frame for a beautiful day.

Something to Try

You can choose just one...

❋ Try changing at least one element of your morning routine and sticking with it for the next few weeks. Maybe set your clock radio fifteen minutes earlier than you do now, and ease yourself more gently into the morning. Or treat yourself to a new CD that has inspirational, peppy morning music.

❋ Plan five healthy breakfast menus. Leslie Sansone, fitness expert and contributing editor to *Woman's Day* magazine, recommends that a healthy, energy-producing breakfast should include a balance of carbohydrates, protein, and fat. One option she suggests is a spoonful of peanut butter on whole-wheat bread with a piece of fruit.[3]

❋ Next weekend pack a simple breakfast picnic and "kidnap" your friend, husband, children, or parents to watch the sunrise. (The element of surprise adds to the celebration!) Declare praise and thanksgiving to the Lord as you admire the beauty of His creation.[4]

17

Sleep Tight

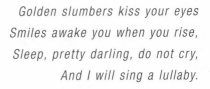

Golden slumbers kiss your eyes
Smiles awake you when you rise,
Sleep, pretty darling, do not cry,
And I will sing a lullaby.

THOMAS DEKKER, ADAPTED

re you tired, weary, worn out? Here's a revolutionary idea: sleep!

Researchers estimate that two-thirds of Americans don't get the sleep they truly need. In this society, where you are respected and rewarded for how much you do, it can just be too tempting to stay up late to finish one more task, then get up early for a good start on the day. The trouble is, you'll usually pay for that decision in terms of weariness and stress.

Our fast-paced, get-more-done, twenty-four-hour lifestyle seems to see sleep as optional, but nothing could be further from the truth. Americans tend to brag about their ability to "get by" on very few hours of slumber, but if you've convinced yourself that you do just fine on four or five hours a night (and sometimes less), think again. Studies have found that sleep-deprived people are more prone to depression and health problems, including diabetes. They are more likely to lose control emotionally and significantly more likely to have accidents.

Your body and mind can function only so long without sufficient restful sleep. How do you make sure you're getting enough? Your answers to the following "three *how*s" can help point you in the right direction and protect you from exhaustion, stress, and burnout.

How Much Do You Sleep?

Sleep is one of your most important daily physical needs, more important than food and exercise. Food is critical, but you could survive for thirty to fifty days without it. Exercise is also valuable, but people do manage to live for years without much of it. If you go longer than thirty-six hours without sleep, however, you will lose your concentration and become emotionally unstable.

Sleep energizes your body, calms your anxieties, refreshes your attitude, and increases your creativity. Arranging your schedule to get at least seven hours each night is one of the best ways to combat weariness.

"But I don't have that much time to waste sleeping," Linda told me (Steve). "I have two young kids, and I work all day. In the evening I have too much to do around the house. Something has to give, and it's usually my rest."

"But you can't afford to cheat sleep," I told her. "Going without it is going to hurt you more than you think. You

deserve your rest. More important, you can't function without it."

"I know," she admitted. "I'm so tired. There are days I
can't even think straight. But I don't know what to do."

You may relate to Linda's dilemma. You may recognize
the importance of sleep but feel you can't do anything
about it—you're just too busy. If you are that busy on a regular basis, we're concerned about you. You were not
designed to function for extended periods without rest. If
your activities are keeping you from getting the sleep you
need, please reconsider what you have squeezed into your
days. Now might be the time to sort out your priorities and
cross a few things off your to-do list.

However, there may well be periods when the legitimate
demands of life keep you from sleeping as long or as well as
you may like. A new baby, a family emergency, or a truly
important project might force you to get less rest for a season. Your body will adjust to periodic shortages, and you
can even "make up" sleep to a certain extent. But if your
sleep deprivation becomes chronic, your body and spirit will
pay the price. And the irony is that most activities you might
miss out on by getting a good night's slumber could be made
up another day with greater efficiency and concentration.

How Well Do You Sleep?

If you've ever spent a night tossing or turning or waking up
every few hours, you know that *how well* you sleep is just

201

as important as *how long* you sleep. When you don't wake up refreshed, it's usually the result of one or more of the following:

* *Disruptive noises:* Barking dogs, snoring partners, and obnoxious faucet drips can drive you nuts. To mask outside noises, consider a CD with soft ocean waves or relaxing music, the "white noise" of an air conditioner, or earplugs. If you have to, go to bed in a different room—or suggest your spouse try one of those simple nose clips that enhance breathing.

* *Physical discomfort:* If you can't physically relax, you can't sleep. Consider whether environmental factors are keeping you awake. Try adjusting the temperature in the room, cracking open a window to ventilate, switching to smoother or softer sheets, or even replacing your mattress or pillows.

* *Medical issues:* During the day you may be so busy and focused that physical pain can be ignored. But at night, your pain becomes more noticeable and, well, more painful. In addition, hormonal changes can lead to disrupted sleep patterns. If this is a problem for you, talk to your primary care physician and ask about pain medication or other treatments.

* *Fears or anxieties:* At night, when all is quiet, your mind is often gripped by the *what ifs*. If you can, distract yourself with positive thoughts. Breathe deeply, pray, consciously turn your worries over to God, and see if sleep will overtake you again. You might also go back and review chapter 14, on worry.

A weary Christian lay awake one night
trying to hold the world together by his worrying.
Then he heard the Lord gently say,
"You can go to sleep now. I'll sit up."

RUTH BELL GRAHAM[5]

Whatever the problem, if you wake in the middle of the night and can't fall back to sleep in less than fifteen minutes, you must do something. The longer you lie there awake, the more frustrated you're likely to be, and this in turn can make it even harder to sleep. Many people have found the following strategies helpful for coping with middle-of-the-night wakefulness:

- Get out of bed, but keep the lights low. (Bright lights tend to stimulate wakefulness.)
- Have a cup of herbal (noncaffeinated) tea, hot water with lemon, or warm milk.
- Read a relaxing, nonstimulating book or calming and reassuring passages from your Bible.
- If problems and worries have been keeping you awake, write them down in a notebook or journal. Deliberately leave them in another room when you return to bed.
- Pray.
- After fifteen minutes, go back to bed.

Most of the time, one or more of these ideas will help you fall back to sleep. If they don't, get up and repeat the process, but this time stay up for a half hour. If you have tried these and are still tossing and turning after more than three nights in a row, talk to your doctor about further remedies.

How Do You Prepare for Sleep?

What you do when you're awake—especially in the evening—can have a significant effect on how long and how well you sleep. That's because whatever is on your mind as you prepare for bed tends to be processed all night. If you have a conflict, you review it. If you had a problem, you try to solve it. If you have a fear, you worry about it.

Sometimes getting to sleep seems impossible. You lie in bed—worn out, exhausted, yearning for rest—but your mind is racing a hundred miles an hour. You check the clock every ten minutes, count sheep until you go crazy, and plan your menus for the next year. And the longer you can't sleep, the more frustrated you get. The greater the frustration, the more adrenaline is pumped through your body, pushing your precious slumber even further away.

I don't know if the apostle Paul was thinking of sleep when he wrote, "Do not let the sun go down on your anger,"[2] but the advice can certainly help. Lingering anger, frustration, and conflicts can either prevent sleep or make slumber uneasy and restless. You can improve your sleep dramatically by resolving such difficulties two to three hours before placing your head on the pillow—or at least making a specific plan to resolve them the next day.

This is also true of solving complicated problems, processing painful memories, or facing fears. These are best done with trusted friends during the day. The evening is the time to gently slow down the body and brain. Rehearsing difficulties does the opposite, arousing your brain instead of relaxing it. If you can't complete these tasks during the day or in the early evening, intentionally put them on hold until the next day. (Some of the "stop worry" strategies from chapter 14 can help you do this.)

One Hour Before Bedtime

- Avoid caffeinated drinks.
- Drink Sleepytime-type teas.
- Turn off TV news or tense dramas.
- Listen to relaxing music.
- Avoid vigorous exercise.
- Take a bubble bath.
- Read something calming or comforting.
- Stop working on energizing projects.
- Put on clothing that is comfortable and cozy.
- Dim the lights.
- Pray.

Whether it's before going to sleep or upon waking up in the middle of the night, prayer can help calm your spirit and relax your body. There is something soothing and comforting about knowing that God understands your every challenge and struggle. King David wrote,

> On my bed I remember you;
>> I think of you through the watches of the night.
> Because you are my help,
>> I sing in the shadow of your wings.
> My soul clings to you;
>> your right hand upholds me.[3]

By knowing that God is in control, you can truly let go and, as the writer of Proverbs says, "your sleep will be sweet."[4]

Sleep Tight!

Parents know how important sleep is for their children. When they are infants, their parents rock them to sleep. When they are toddlers, their parents sing lullabies or buy restful CDs. When they are grade schoolers, their parents create all sorts of rituals, from reading their favorite books to checking under their bed for monsters to saying nighttime prayers—all to help their children calm down and fall asleep. Even when they are teenagers, their parents set curfews and bedtimes in an attempt to help their offspring get enough sleep.

Parents recognize that without good enough rest, their kids will not have a good day. This wise principle is just as important to adults as it is to children. When I (Steve) was a child, my mother used to tuck me into bed each night and then say in a soft and tender voice, "Sleep tight." With these two words, I knew everything was okay and I could close my eyes, letting go of all the cares and worries of the day.

Tonight treat yourself to that same kind of gentle love. Slip into bed, find that perfect cozy and comfortable position, push away all the difficulties of the day, and close your eyes. (You might even want to put on a CD and play yourself a lullaby.) Remember that your heavenly Father is watching—and that, in the words of the psalmist, He "never tires and never sleeps."[5]

Then, as you start to relax, imagine a gentle embrace and a soft whisper with those nurturing words "Sleep tight."

Something to Try

You can choose just one...

* If you usually watch television right up to bedtime, try turning it off early and listening to soothing music instead. Experiment for five nights in a row and see if this helps you fall asleep more peacefully.

* When worries visit you in the nighttime, try singing "Jesus Loves Me" in your mind. Imagine that He is rocking you to sleep as you sing.

* Try to make your bedroom an inviting and relaxing place. Look to see if there are easy ways to unclutter the area. Visit a "bed and bath" store and look for a pretty bed throw or a new pillow.

* Take your favorite essential oil (vanilla, peach, and rose are all nice for this purpose) and rub it on the light bulbs in your bedroom and on night-lights. The room will be infused with a gentle scent as the light heats up the oil. You can buy already prepared plug-in fragrances, but doing it yourself is more fun.

18

So Much Beauty

I don't ask for the meaning
of the song of a bird
or the rising of the sun on a misty morning.
There they are,
and they are beautiful.

PETE HAMILL

y wife, Tami, had been in the house just a few minutes before, but now she seemed to have disappeared. Our children looked in each room, and finally the youngest went outside and called at the top of his voice, "MOOOOMMM!"

"Here I am," replied Tami, stepping out from between the sunflowers and calla lilies of her garden retreat.

We aren't surprised when we find her there. Whenever Tami gets worn out, overloaded, or just needs a breath of fresh air, she retreats to the well-tended beauty of our backyard. She says that a few minutes surrounded by plants, flowers, and trees give her the boost she needs to make it through the rest of the day.

Beauty is a very dependable antidote to stress and weariness. We say that with all seriousness.

There is a great deal of plainness and ugliness in all our lives. Yet we are also surrounded by beauty, much of which goes unnoticed because we are so busy scrambling from point *A* to point *B*.

About once a week, someone who has been to my (Steve's) office many times will look at the prints on my wall and say something like, "When did you get those new pictures? They're beautiful." I try to respond graciously, but the truth is that those "new pictures" have been there for nearly ten years. Most of us just don't see what is good and peaceful and lovely all around us.

We need beauty to pull us above the difficulties and drudgery of everyday existence. If we let it, beauty will touch our soul and lift our attitude, helping us feel more positive and less exhausted.

Jesus said, "Seek and you will find."[1] This is true of many things, even beauty. If you don't seek it out, you may not find it, even when it's all around you. But if you are looking, it's amazing how *much* you can find. Suddenly life is not as dull or difficult as you thought.

Jen didn't realize all she was missing until she took a class on the Japanese tea ceremony. The class met in a serene garden, and one of her first assignments was to focus—really focus—on an ancient, twisted tree. She was to study its shape and size, follow its outline, and dwell on its symmetry; examine the trunk, limbs, and leaves; consider the texture and color of each part, noticing the various shadings and hues.

"I thought this would be the most boring thing I've ever done," Jen told me later. "After all, I've seen thousands of trees in my life, and a tree is just a tree. But after about five minutes I started seeing all sorts of detail I had never noticed before."

Beauty needs to be seen to be appreciated, and as the old saying goes, "So many look, but so few see." Opening your eyes to what is lovely around you is a very practical way to reduce your weariness. Try to see with your spirit and let beauty touch your heart. Absorb it and let it soothe away your tension. Let it slow you down and soften the rough edges of your life. Beauty brings peace and pleasure. The longer you enjoy it, the less worn out you will feel.

211

The Beauty of Nature

Nature has a different pace that draws you to it. As I write this, I'm watching giant waves crash onto the rugged rocks of the Oregon coast. In the distance, whales arch and spout with a gracefulness that belies their size. The steady roar is somehow calming, and the power and splendor of the scene captivates me. I could sit here all day.

One cannot collect all the beautiful shells on the beach. One can collect only a few and they are more beautiful if they are few.

ANNE MORROW LINDBERGH[2]

I (Steve) am a beach person. Some people love the desert, while others love the forest. A friend of mine enjoys the high mountains, with their icy solitude and magnificent views. Another friend loves the flowers and trees and grass of a finely landscaped city park. God has created such a variety of beauty that it is present wherever you go. Even when I was in northern Iceland, near the Arctic Circle, I was surprised to find so much incredible beauty surrounding me—breathtaking waterfalls, midnight sun, summer wildflowers, jagged mountains, and bubbling hot springs.

God's awesome imagination is written all over nature. One hot summer night when our family was camping, I whispered to my nine-year-old son, Dylan, to look up. Since we live where the city lights seem to dim the heavenly ones, I was not surprised when he looked up and gasped, "WOW!" With head tilted up, he turned a slow circle, mesmerized by the stars that seemed almost close enough to touch.

As a kid I too was mesmerized by the infinite twinkling of a starry night. Sunsets are another miracle, with reds and yellows and purples painting magic on the western horizon.

God's natural creation changes from season to season—and from region to region. In Oregon, where I live, spring brings green buds to the trees, music of birds to the air, and warm showers that invite bright flowers to blossom. Beneath the clear blue summer skies, fruit ripens to delicious perfection. Cool autumn evenings leave their frosty touch on the pumpkins, and the trees blaze bright in a burst of glory. Then days grow shorter and colder as leaves fall, clouds conceal the sun, and the earth begins her winter rest under a silent cloak of snow.

In Arizona, where Alice lives, the flow of the seasons is different but just as incredible—the cool sunshine of winter days, the wonder of desert life blossoming suddenly after spring showers, the pale colors of a sun-baked summer day, and the silhouettes of palm trees against the bright blue autumn sky.

The beauty of God's creation is inescapable—if we only open our eyes (and other senses) to appreciate it. More important, it's a reminder of God's amazing and ingenious provision for us, that He gives us not only basic food and shelter, but also a world overwhelming with spirit-lifting wonder.

The Beauty of Art, Music, and Literature

Enjoying artistic beauty is another way of healing all that is worn out in our spirits. Art in its purest sense is an attempt to duplicate or describe some aspect of God's creation. My dictionary defines it as "human works of beauty—from dance to drawing to drama to sculpture." In whatever form, artistic beauty lifts you above the ordinary and provides a break from the hectic.

Every worn-out woman is unique, of course. Just as different aspects of nature draw us differently, we are drawn to different kinds of art. I like to ask my clients what type of visual art touches their sense of beauty, and I am fascinated by the variety of response. Many are drawn to landscapes, seascapes, pictures of flowers and old houses. Some love portraits, especially of children. Others are drawn to impressionist swirls of color or the power of stylized compositions. My friend Julie loves to find a quiet place and read her garden magazines because the colors, textures, and designs of the photographic layouts trigger her imagination and inspire her.

Someone recently said that music provides the sound track of one's life. Whether it's jazz, praise, gospel, folk, Celtic, country, rock, or classical, music can provide a touchstone—a reminder of who we are and where we've been. It can also have a powerful effect on how we feel, either energizing us or relaxing us.

The Bible tells of a time when King Saul became disturbed and out of control—perhaps overloaded with worries and work. But his servants asked David to play the harp for him, and Saul was able to relax.[3] I know plenty of tense women who have found that soothing music is a good way to cover the stress-producing noises that so easily put us on edge. A headset filled with beautiful music can muffle the loudness of the outside world and return gentleness to your soul.

For many worn-out women, of course, nothing is more relaxing than a good book. Something that is well written and attractively designed can delight the mind and enchant the emotions. Tenderly written words carry a sweetness that wash away cares and concerns. Beautiful words in beautiful books are treasures to which we can return time and time again.

While we are considering art, it's worth noting that the act of *creating* it can be as soothing or uplifting as the act of enjoying it. Being made in God's image means we were made to create beauty, and many women have found that artistic pursuits can be fulfilling, uplifting, and therapeutic.

A friend of mine who is taking a pottery class informs me that working with the clay helps her feel "grounded." Another woman loves going to the ballet and has begun taking classes. A third has recently started writing poetry. All of these women have discovered that their quest to create beauty not only enriches their lives, but also makes them feel years younger.

215

The Five Senses

Whenever stress and turmoil start to strangle you, try concentrating on your five senses. Focusing on the physical realities around you—experiencing them through sight, sound, taste, smell, and touch—is a wonderful way to still the racing of your heart.

See the full moon standing strong against a canopy of sparkling stars or a photograph of a brilliant rainbow arching over places you've never been. *Hear* the rhythm of bubbling water in a fountain or the familiar melodies of your favorite songs. *Feel* the softness of a newborn baby's face or the smooth cold marble of a finely chiseled sculpture. *Smell* the clean scent of the forest after a summer's rain or the aroma of freshly baked bread. *Taste* the sweetness of a juicy strawberry or the lingering richness of a dark chocolate truffle.

A More Beautiful Life—Some Simple Suggestions

- Go outside! Just a daily walk in the park or the neighborhood can lower your stress levels.

- Bring natural beauty into your home with flowers and greenery—an easy-to-grow houseplant, a bouquet from the supermarket, or even a dandelion in a jar.

- If you live in an area you don't think is beautiful, ask God to refocus your eyes to appreciate subtle or hidden beauty around you—a flower in a crevice, a neatly plowed field, a carefully tended tree in an industrial park.

- Invest in a piece of artwork you *really* like—a picture, a small sculpture, a quilt. Put it in a spot where you will see it every day.

- Take a child to a museum or a concert and enjoy rediscovering beauty through his or her eyes and ears.

- Find a book about an artist, writer, or composer you admire and keep it at your bedside.

- Take a music break. Put on a favorite CD or tune the radio to a favorite station. Close your eyes and enjoy—or get up and dance.

- Turn off the TV and radio and take a silence break. Just sit quietly for fifteen minutes and try to identify the various sounds that reach your ears.

- Schedule an afternoon of browsing in a bookstore

that allows you to sit and read, preferably with a cup of tea from the coffee shop.

✳ Is there a creative pursuit you "used to do" but haven't had time for in recent years? Pull out the guitar or the sewing machine or the sculpting tools, and mark off time in your schedule for rediscovery.

✳ Choose an herb or spice you've never used before and learn to use it in your cooking. When you eat out, try to detect the presence of your "new" flavor.

✳ Buy or sew a pillow or throw in a really luscious fabric—cool, smooth cotton; velvety chenille; or cozy flannel. Enjoy cuddling up to something that delights your sense of touch.

One of the delights of focusing on what our senses reveal is that doing so keeps us anchored in the here and now—and that in turn keeps us from obsessing about the past or the future. It's hard to live thankfully in the present and still worry about what happened yesterday or what might happen tomorrow.

But the beauty we experience with our senses need not be limited just to the moment. Our memories of beauty can also be powerful tools to keep stress at bay. I believe we should make a point of holding the lovely moments of our lives in memory so we can enjoy them again and again when life seems bleak. With one cold, rainy day we forget all the warmth and wonder of a sunny summer—or we forget the silvery beauty of a rainy afternoon when the sun is baking and graying the landscape. We need to nurture our memories so the beauty we have known in the past is not lost to us. It remains as a source of hope and encouragement when life becomes difficult.

I have just spent the most wonderful and relaxing weekend with my family at the Oregon coast. As I write, the sun is setting into a stormy sea. The crashing of the surf sets a soothing rhythm to the weekend. In the last few days we have walked barefoot in the fine gray sand with the wind at our faces, lingered over delicious food, and enjoyed the brisk, fresh smell of the ocean. I feel more peaceful and at ease than I have in weeks.

Tomorrow I must return to the city. Responsibilities and obligations wait in an unsavory plot to wear me out. But though I must return to stacks of unfinished work, I will often recall that beautiful weekend by the sea, and those wonderful memories will help provide the refreshment I need.

Surely beauty strengthens us through our hectic days. So seek it wherever you can. Nurture its presence in your life. Cherish it as a refreshing gift from the Lord who loves you. As we write these last few lines, we are praying that you will discover that your path from worn-out to winsome is sprinkled with many moments of beauty.

Something to Try

You can choose just one...

❋ Take a nature walk and explore the simple pleasure of being outside. Listen to the birds, the wind, and your thoughts. Reach down to feel the texture of the grass, leaves, and soil. Consciously savor the beauty of God's creation in the specific place where you live.

❋ Have you ever wanted to try an artistic pursuit? Look for a way to do it now while the desire is strong. A good first step is researching the possibilities. Often community colleges offer classes in watercolor painting, pottery, creative writing, playing an instrument, or even modern dance.

❋ Visit an art museum or art gallery near where you live. Try to plan a lazy weekend afternoon when you can leisurely enjoy the gift of artistic expression.

❋ If your community has a local pond or lake, take a loaf of bread and feed the ducks. Or step outside your door and blow some bubbles. As you watch them float upward, notice the rainbows in their spheres.

❋ We would enjoy hearing about your journey from worn out to winsome. Please take a moment to visit us at www.thewornoutwoman.com or drop a note c/o Multnomah Publishers, P.O. Box 1720, Sisters, OR 97759.

❋ In the meantime, throw some confetti and celebrate!

Ideas for a Friendship (Study) Group

Elizabeth Barrett Browning once asked Charles Kingsley the secret of his happy life. He replied simply, "I have a friend." Whether it's going out for a latte, taking a walk in the early morning sunshine, or reading a good book—most things are better when shared with a friend.

If you want to make your experience of reading this book richer, perhaps you will choose to journey through it with a friend, a book club, or a Bible friendship group. The section at the end of each chapter called, "Something to Try" will be fun to discuss with others. For those who wish to share on a little deeper level, we are including some additional questions and ideas for each chapter. If your group wants to move at a faster pace, the chapters are short enough to do more than one each week.

Two people can accomplish more than twice as much as one; they get a better return for their labor.

ECCLESIASTES 4:9

Prologue: Winter Night

1. During what periods of your life have you been the most worn out?

2. Do you think you're a worn-out woman now?

3. How did you feel on your worst days?

4. How did you get to the place of being so worn out?

Chapter 1: What's Going On?

1. When you feel the symptoms on pages 24–25, what negative emotions or thought patterns do you experience?

2. Describe some of the ways you tend to treat others when you are worn out.

   How do they respond to you?

   How do you feel about this?

3. What are some of the ways you try to take care of your own needs?

Chapter 2: Telling Your Story

1. What aspects of your personality make you more or less vulnerable to being worn out?

2. What were some of the high and low points of your life?

   Share some of the ways the high points affected your life.

   Share some of the ways the low points affected your faith.

3. Think back to the times in your life when you have felt worn out.

How long did these times last?

How did you get out of them?

Chapter 3: Shoulds and Oughts

1. What are some of the *ought*s and *should*s you struggle with the most? Where do you think these came from?

2. In what areas of life are you most likely to compare yourself with others?

3. What is the difference between people pleasing and being unselfish? How can you strive for one without falling into the other?

Chapter 4: Time for a Change

1. What are some areas of commitment where you said yes but now wish you had said no?

2. Once you have said yes to a commitment, how can you gracefully and responsibly make a reversal?

3. Tell about a time when you said no and are thankful that you did.

Chapter 5: Playing to Your Strengths

1. How have others described your strengths and gifts? Do you agree? (Note: If the women in the group know each other well, take some time to describe each other's strengths and gifts.)

2. In what ways are you already using your gifts and strengths? In what ways are you working/serving in areas outside of your gifts and strengths?

3. What are some ways you can transition toward playing

to your strengths? Are there some ways this group can help with your transition?

Chapter 6: When Your Lamp Burns Low

1. Describe the most refreshing or renewing mini-retreat you have ever taken. If you have never taken a mini-retreat, describe what you would like to do.

2. What are your current energy drainers?

   How long have you struggled with them?

   What can you do to change them?

3. Reread the paragraph on page 78 about Dr. Ogilvie. What kind of wonderful woman do you think God had in mind when He created you?

Chapter 7: Face to the Sunshine

1. Share some of the things you do to help you keep a positive attitude.

   What usually helps the most?

   What else could you try?

2. What events are most likely to cause you to slip into a negative mood? What helps you get out of it?

3. Name one or two people you consider to be a blessing in your life. Tell some of the ways you show your appreciation for them.

Chapter 8: Yellow Umbrellas

1. In what areas of your life or in what specific situations do you need the most encouragement? What usually helps you the most?

Positive words

Hugs and physical touch

Action and assistance

2. Describe one of the nicest acts of kindness someone has done for you. How did you react?

3. Recall a time when you were blessed by doing something kind for someone else. What did you do? How did the other person respond?

Chapter 9: The Secret of Simplicity

1. How would you describe the mental, emotional, and spiritual clutter that fills your soul right now? Name one specific step you can take to clean up this clutter.

2. Mentally review your schedule this week. Try to name one item that can be delegated to someone else, changed to a more convenient time, or omitted altogether. If you are having trouble delegating, does someone in the group have some helpful ideas? Does someone in your friendship group want to try some job sharing or chore trading?

3. Which room in your living space is most cluttered? What is preventing you from cleaning it up? How can someone in this group help you?

Chapter 10: Soul Nurturing

1. When is the best and most practical time of the day for you to nurture your soul? What are some of the things that distract you or prevent you from keeping this time protected and meaningful?

2. Tell about a book you have read that inspired you and strengthened your spiritual life.

3. When you think about journaling, what thoughts and feelings come to you?

> If you have kept a journal, describe how often you wrote, what you wrote about, and how the act of journaling affected you.

> If you have not kept a journal yourself, do you know someone who journals on a regular basis? How does this enrich her life?

Chapter 11: You Gotta Have Friends

1. What do you treasure the most from your friends?

> Perspective
>
> Company
>
> A place to vent
>
> Accountability
>
> Encouragement
>
> Wisdom
>
> Shared interests
>
> Other

2. Describe the friend(s) you go to when you are most worn out. What do they provide that your other friends do not?

3. In what ways can being worn out hurt a friendship? How can you prevent this?

Chapter 12: Burlap People

1. When you think of the difficult people currently in your life, how do they remind you of past difficult people? How did you deal with difficult people from your past?

2. What lessons do you think God may be trying to teach you through the difficult people in your life?

3. Share how you plan to deal with them in a way that is wise, loving, and healthy.

Chapter 13: The Gift of Forgiveness

1. Why do you think God's forgiveness of us is connected with our forgiveness of others?

2. What is the hardest kind of offense for you to forgive? What "potatoes" do you tend to hold on to and carry around?

3. Which of the following steps to forgiveness is (or might be) the most difficult for you and why?

   Admitting your hurts and anger

   Remembering why forgiveness is important

   Talking it out with the person who hurt you

   Choosing forgiveness

   Putting the hurt behind you

   Being patient with the process

   Forgiving yourself

Chapter 14: Worry Is a Rocking Chair

1. Which areas of your body are usually most affected by worry? Describe the symptoms you typically notice in your:

Stomach

Head

Eyes

Jaw

Neck/shoulder

Leg muscles

Chest/heart

2. Under what circumstances are you most prone to worry?

3. What has been your most effective strategy to date for reducing worry?

Chapter 15: When Dreams Shatter

1. What keeps you from coming to and leaning on God? How can you get rid of these blocks?

2. If you looked at your life from God's perspective, what would you see?

What pleases Him?

What would He want to change to make your life fuller, richer, and more satisfying?

3. How can others in this friendship group help you get C-L-O-S-E-R to God?

Chapter 16: Starting Your Day Right

1. What makes you think of yourself as "a morning person" or "a night person"?

2. Describe your usual morning routine. Does it help reduce your stress or contribute to it?

3. After reading this chapter, what is one thing you would like to change about your morning routine? Is someone in your friendship group willing to keep you accountable for doing this the next two weeks?

Chapter 17: Sleep Tight

1. If your parents created a positive bedtime ritual when you were a little girl, tell what you remember about it. If you have children, what bedtime ritual have you established with them?

2. Describe your own current nighttime routine.

> How fast do you usually go to sleep?
>
> What keeps you awake?
>
> What usually helps you fade into sleep?
>
> What are some of your favorite helps for getting a good night's sleep?

3. After reading this chapter, what is one thing you might change about your nighttime routine?

Chapter 18: So Much Beauty

1. Describe a favorite place that touches you with the beauty of God's creation.

2. Name at least one aspect of each season of the year that gives it its own amazing beauty. Which season is your favorite and why?

3. What kinds of art, music, and literature either relax or energize you?

LISTS TO LIVE BY FOR EVERY MARRIED COUPLE

Offers tender, romantic, and wise ways to bring new life to marriage in a popular, easy-to-read format! This special collection of *Lists to Live By* is filled with gems of inspiration and timeless truths that married couples will treasure for a lifetime.
ISBN 1-57673-998-8

LISTS TO LIVE BY FOR EVERY CARING FAMILY

Provides inspiration on how to love, teach, understand, uplift, and communicate with children in topics such as "Helping Your Child Succeed," "Pray for Your Children," and "Four Ways to Encourage Your Kids." Parents will cherish each nugget of truth in this timeless special collection of *Lists to Live By*.
ISBN 1-57673-999-6

LISTS TO LIVE BY FOR SIMPLE LIVING

In our fast-paced, complex world, we all are looking for stillness, harmony, gentleness, and peace. The beauty of these eighty thoughtfully chosen lists is that they use simplicity to bring you simplicity—condensing essential information into one- or two-page lists.
ISBN 1-59052-058-0

LISTS TO LIVE BY FOR SMART LIVING

Reading a list is like having the best parts of a whole book gathered into a few words. Each list is a simple path to a better—smarter—life! If you read them, use them, and live them, you will become successful where it really matters—family, friendship, health, finance, business, wisdom, and faith.
ISBN 1-59052-057-2

To learn more visit: www.multnomahbooks.com

Life-Changing Advice in a Quick-to-Read Format!
LISTS TO LIVE BY

LISTS TO LIVE BY

This treasury of to-the-point inspiration—two hundred lists—is loaded with invaluable insights for wives, husbands, kids, teens, friends, and more. These wide-ranging ideas can change your life!
ISBN 1-57673-478-1

LISTS TO LIVE BY: THE SECOND COLLECTION

You'll get a lift in a hurry as you browse through this treasure-trove of more *Lists to Live By*—with wisdom for home, health, love, life, faith, and successful living.
ISBN 1-57673-685-7

LISTS TO LIVE BY: THE THIRD COLLECTION

Two hundred lists with power wisdom, inspiration, and practical advice. Some will make you reflect. Some will make you smile. Some will move you to action.
ISBN 1-57673-882-5

LISTS TO LIVE BY: THE FOURTH COLLECTION

This bestselling series returns with a fourth collection of two hundred powerful lists on success, simplicity, love, faith, parenting, retirement, wisdom, and more.
ISBN 1-59052-059-9

The Walk Out Woman

by Dr. Steve Stephens & Alice Gray

Coming Summer 2004

Every woman longs to be appreciated, respected, noticed, and adored. When she isn't, she could be tempted to walk away from her marriage.

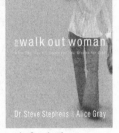

Unaware of how great her loneliness has become, she has distanced herself, losing hope that her marriage can be restored.

But even when hope seems lost, a tiny strand lingers. And the key for any woman who is tempted to walk away is to find that golden strand of hope that will help her and her husband find the way to becoming one again.

If both partners are willing to work at it, any marriage can be saved.

If you are a woman, we pray that you will recognize the symptoms and dangers of becoming a walk away woman and that you will realize it is not a path to happiness. We ask you to open your heart to your marriage again. If you are a man, we pray that you will learn to understand your wife's needs and that you will begin meeting them with the power of selfless love. We hope you will fight for your marriage."

—*Dr. Steve Stephens and Alice Gray*

The Stories for the Heart Series

• More than 5 million sold in series!
• #1-selling Christian Stories series!

www.storiesfortheheart.com
For more information about Alice Gray, visit:
www.alicegray.com

Recommended Reading

For More Help

The books in this section cover a wide range of subjects such as practicing simplicity, letting go of disappointment, nurturing your spirit, and finding more hours in your day. If you want additional help for the topics covered in *The Worn Out Woman,* these books are a great resource.

Andersen, Linda. *Interludes: A Busy Woman's Invitation to Personal and Spiritual Rest.* Colorado Springs, CO: Waterbrook, 2001.

Curtis, Brent, and John Eldredge. *The Sacred Romance: Drawing Closer to the Heart of God.* Nashville, TN: Thomas Nelson, 1997.

Decker, Dru Scott. *Finding More Time in Your Life: With Wisdom from the Bible and Tools That Fit Your Personality.* Eugene, OR: Harvest House, 2001.

Dillow, Linda. *Calm My Anxious Heart: A Woman's Guide to Contentment.* Colorado Springs, CO: Navpress, 1998.

Farrar, Steve, and Mary. *Overcoming Overload: Seven Ways to Find Rest in Your Chaotic World.* Sisters, OR: Multnomah, 2003.

George, Elizabeth. *Life Management for Busy Women: Living Out God's Plan with Passion and Purpose.* Eugene, OR: Harvest House, 2002.

Gray, Alice, Steve Stephens, and John Van Diest. *Lists to Live By for Simple Living.* Sisters, OR: Multnomah, 2002.

Hoffman, Sharon. *Come Home to Comfort: Bringing Hope, Happiness, and Harmony to Today's Busy Woman.* Green Forest, AR: New Leaf Press, 2003.

Johnson, Nicole. *Fresh-Brewed Life: A Stirring Invitation to Wake Up Your Soul.* Nashville, TN: Thomas Nelson, 2001.

Kent, Carol. *Secret Longings of the Heart: Overcoming Deep Disappointment and Unfulfilled Expectations.* Colorado Springs, CO: Navpress, 1992.

McGinnis, Alan Loy. *The Friendship Factor: How to Get Closer to the People You Care For.* Minneapolis, MN: Augsburg Fortress, 1979.

McMenamin, Cindi. *Heart Hunger: Letting God Meet Your Emotional Needs.* Eugene, OR: Harvest House, 2000.

Otto, Donna. *Finding a Mentor, Being a Mentor: Sharing Our Lives as Women of God.* Eugene, OR: Harvest House, 2001.

Otto, Donna. *Get More Done in Less Time—And Get On with the Good Stuff.* Eugene, OR: Harvest House, 1995.

Reeve, Pamela. *Deserts of the Heart: Finding God During the Dry Times.* Sisters, OR: Multnomah, 2001.

Smedes, Lewis B. *Forgive and Forget: Healing the Hurts We Don't Deserve.* Reprint. San Francisco: HarperSan Francisco, 1996.

Stack, Debi. *Martha to the Max: Balanced Living for Perfectionists.* Chicago: Moody, 2001.

Thomas, Kim. *Even God Rested: Why It's Okay for Women to Slow Down.* Eugene, OR: Harvest House, 2003.

Tirabassi, Becky. *Change Your Life: Achieve a Healthy Body, Heal Relationships and Connect with God.* New York: Berkley Publishing Group, 2001.

Vredevelt, Pam. *Letting Go of Worry and Anxiety.* Sisters, OR: Multnomah, 2001.

Vredevelt, Pam. *Letting Go of Disappointments and Painful Losses.* Sisters, OR: Multnomah, 2001.

Waggoner, Brenda. *The Velveteen Woman: Becoming Real*

Through God's Transforming Love. Colorado Springs, CO: Chariot Victor, 2002.

Weaver, Joanna. *Having a Mary Heart in a Martha World.* Revised. Colorado Springs, CO: Waterbrook, 2002.

West, Kari. *Dare to Trust, Dare to Hope Again: Living with Losses of the Heart.* Colorado Springs, CO: Chariot Victor, 2001.

Wilkinson, Bruce. *The Dream Giver: Following Your God-Given Destiny.* Sisters, OR: Multnomah, 2003.

Wilson, Mimi, and Shelly Cook Volkhardt. *Holy Habits: A Woman's Guide to Intentional Living.* Colorado Springs, CO: Navpress, 1999.

Yancey, Philip. *Disappointment with God: Three Questions No One Asks Aloud.* Grand Rapids, MI: Zondervan, 1988.

For Daily Uplift

There are so many wonderful devotional books that it is hard to choose just a few. These are the ones we return to again and again. Our copies have worn pages with lots of underlining and penciled notes in the margins. We think they are perfect for your morning quiet time or for reading right before you turn the light out at night.

Brownlow, LeRoy. *A Psalm in My Heart.* Fort Worth, TX: Brownlow, 1989.

Spurgeon, Charles Haddon. *Beside Still Waters: Words of Comfort for the Soul,* edited by Roy H. Clarke. Nashville, TN: Nelson Reference, 1999.

Cowman, L. B. *Streams in the Desert: 366 Daily Devotional Readings.* Revised edition, edited by James Reimann. Grand Rapids, MI: Zondervan, 1999.

Galvin, James C., Linda Chaffee Taylor, and David R. Veerman. *One Year with Jesus NLT: 365 Daily Devotions.* Wheaton, IL: Tyndale House, 2000.

Keller, Weldon Phillip. *A Shepherd Looks at Psalm 23: An Inspiring and Insightful Guide to One of the Best-Loved Bible Passages.* Grand Rapids, MI: Zondervan, 1997.

Myers, Ruth, and Warren. *31 Days of Praise: Enjoying God Anew.* Sisters, OR: Multnomah, 2002.

Omartian, Stormie. *The Power of a Praying Woman.* Eugene, OR: Harvest House, 2002.

For Fun and Relaxation (and Some Inspiration, Too)

For relieving stress, nothing beats a good story. Fiction may not cure the worn-out woman syndrome, but it can provide a wonderful respite for a weary spirit as well as some insights about how to live wisely and well. The following series of books are time-tested and worn-out-woman-approved.

Gunn, Robin Jones. The Glenbrooke Series: *Secrets, Whispers, Echoes, Sunsets, Clouds, Waterfalls, Woodlands, Wildflowers.* Sisters, OR: Multnomah.

Karon, Jan. Mitford Series: *At Home in Mitford; A Light in the Window; These High, Green Hills; Out to Canaan; A New Song; A Common Life; In This Mountain; Shepherds Abiding.* New York: Penguin USA.

Oke, Janette. Love Comes Softly Series: *Love Comes Softly, Love's Enduring Promise, Love's Long Journey, Love's Abiding Joy, Love's Unending Legacy, Love's Unfolding Dream, Love Takes Wing, Love Finds a Home.* Minneapolis, MN: Bethany House.

Notes

Prologue

1. Dawn Miller, *The Journal of Callie Wade* (New York: Pocket Books, 1996).

Chapter 2: Telling Your Story

1. Psalm 139:3–16. Note: The issue of personality/temperament has fascinated people for thousands of years, and theories of personality abound. Some of the more popular models in the past half-century include the "humors" model explained by writers such as Tim LaHaye and Florence Littauer as well as the popular Myers-Briggs test, the Keirsey-Bates instrument, the DISC model, and so on. If you are interested in finding out more about personality/temperament, we suggest consulting several different books or, even better, a trusted counselor or teacher.
2. Edith Schaeffer, *The Hidden Art of Homemaking* (Wheaton, IL: Tyndale House, 1971), 128–30.
3. Song of Solomon 2:4, NIV.

Chapter 3: Shoulds and Oughts

1. Romans 12:3, Phillips.
2. See Psalm 139:13–16; John 3:16; 1 Peter 5:7.
3. Mary Lyn Miller, "Finding My Passion," in *Chicken Soup for the Surviving Soul: 101 Stories of Courage and Inspiration from Those Who Have Survived Cancer* (Deerfield Beach, FL: Health Communications, 1996), as posted on the website for Mary Lyn Miller's Life & Career Clinic, http://www.l-cc.com/press_soup.htm, copyright Mary Lyn Miller 2002.
4. 1 Thessalonians 2:4.

Chapter 4: Time for a Change

1. Psalm 23:2–3, NIV.

Chapter 5: Playing to Your Strengths

1. Max Lucado, *Just Like Jesus* (Nashville, TN: Word, 1998), 96.
2. Patrick Kavanaugh, *You Are Talented!* (Grand Rapids, MI: Chosen, 2002), 17–8.
3. Nicole Johnson, *Fresh-Brewed Life: A Stirring Invitation to Wake Up Your Soul* (Nashville, TN: Thomas Nelson, 2001).
4. Romans 12:3–12, NIV.
5. Matthew 25:21, 23, NIV.

Chapter 6: When Your Lamp Burns Low

1. Adapted from a story told by John Maxwell in *Developing the Leader Within You* (Nashville, TN: Thomas Nelson, 1993), 29. Also told by Max Lucado in

Just Like Jesus (Nashville, TN: Word, 1998), 97. This is my retelling, not Maxwell's or Lucado's.

2. Adapted from Anne Graham Lotz, *Just Give Me Jesus* (Nashville, TN: Word, 2000), 172.
3. Ephesians 5:17, TLB.
4. Jean Fleming, *Between Walden and the Whirlwind* (Colorado Springs, CO: Navpress, 1985).

Chapter 7: Face to the Sunshine

1. Charles R. Swindoll, *Strengthening Your Grip* (Waco, TX: Word, 1986).
2. Margery Silver and Thomas Perls, *Living to 100: Lessons in Living to Your Maximum Potential at Any Age* (New York: Basic, 2000).
3. Proverbs 23:7, NKJV.
4. Philippians 4:8, NIV.
5. Proverbs 17:22.
6. Paul Meyer, *Unlocking Your Legacy* (Chicago: Moody, 2002), 224.
7. "Count Your Blessings," Johnson Oatman Jr. (text) and Edwin O. Excell (music), 1897.
8. Psalm 107:1; 118:1; 136:1, NIV.
9. Nancie Carmody, *Family Circle,* November 16, 1999, 21.
10. Excerpted from Alice Gray, Steve Stephens, John Van Diest, comp., *Lists to Live By for Simple Living* (Sisters, OR: Multnomah, 2002), 78. Used by permission of the author.

Chapter 8: Yellow Umbrellas

1. Acts 20:35, *The Message.*
2. Gary Smalley and John Trent, *Leaving the Light On* (Sisters, OR: Multnomah, 1994).
3. Adapted from Susannah Seton, Robert Taylor, and David Greer, comp., *Simple Pleasures* (Berkeley, CA: Conari Press, 1996), 194.

Chapter 9: The Secret of Simplicity

1. Anne Morrow Lindbergh, *Gift from the Sea* (New York: Random House, 1955, 1975), 19, 21.
2. Psalm 51:10.
3. Matthew 6:19.
4. Randy Alcorn, *The Treasure Principle* (Sisters, OR: Multnomah, 2001), 53–4.
5. We suggest Donna Otto's *Get More Done in Less Time* (Eugene, OR: Harvest House, 1995).

Chapter 10: Soul Nurturing

1. Richard A. Swenson, *Margin: Restoring Emotional, Physical, Financial, and Time Reserves to Overloaded Lives* (Colorado Springs, CO: Navpress, 1995).
2. Psalm 42:1, NIV.

3. Barbara Curtis, "Chapel of the Wash and Dry," in Jack Canfield et al., eds., *Chicken Soup for the Christian Woman's Soul: Stories to Open the Heart and Rekindle the Spirit* (Deerfield Beach, FL: Health Communications, 2002), 362.

4. Rhonda D. Byrd, "The Year at-a-Glance!" *Women's Ministry Network,* December 12, 2002. http://www.womensministry.net/IdeaBank/resultsoutreach.htm (accessed September 30, 2003).

5. Pamela Reeve, *Faith Is* (Sisters, OR: Multnomah, 1970).

6. Kathy Callahan-Howell, "Mary Heart, Martha Brain," *Leadership* 23, no. 4 (Fall 2001): 56.

7. Joanna Bloss, "Spiritually Dry," *Virtue* December 1999/January 2000, 51.

8. Ruth Bell Graham, *Legacy of a Pack Rat* (Nashville, TN: Thomas Nelson, 1989), 53.

9. Carole Mayhall, *When God Whispers: Glimpses of an Extraordinary God by an Ordinary Woman* (Colorado Springs, CO: Navpress, 1994), 15.

Chapter 11: You Gotta Have Friends

1. Condensed from "Five Ways to Find a Friend," *Today's Christian Woman* 23, no. 2 (March/April 2001): 56. Used by permission of the author.

2. 1 Corinthians 13:7.

3. Ecclesiastes 4:9–10, 12.

Chapter 12: Burlap People

1. Ephesians 4:15, NIV.

2. Matthew 5:44.

Chapter 13: The Gift of Forgiveness

1. Walter Wangerin Jr., *As for Me and My House* (Nashville, TN: Thomas Nelson, 1987), 97.

2. Ephesians 4:32, NASB, emphasis mine.

3. 1 John 1:9.

4. Ken Sande, *The Peacemaker,* 2nd ed. (Grand Rapids, MI: Baker, 1997), 189–90.

5. Included in Robert Boyd Munger, *What Jesus Says* (Ada, MI: Revell, 1955).

Chapter 14: Worry Is a Rocking Chair

1. Dale Carnegie, *How to Stop Worrying and Start Living* (New York: Simon & Schuster, 1944), 60.

2. Matthew 6:25, 34.

3. Joanna Weaver, *Having a Mary Heart in a Martha World* (Colorado Springs, CO: Waterbrook, 2000).

4. Expanded from a prayer originally given in a radio broadcast around 1944.

5. Donna Otto, *Get More Done in Less Time* (Eugene, OR: Harvest House, 1995), 30.

6. 1 Peter 5:7.
7. Philippians 4:7.

Chapter 15: When Dreams Shatter

1. Psalm 30:5.
2. See Psalm 56:8 in the NASB, NLT, or KJV. Other versions translate this verse differently, stating that God has written our tears on a scroll. It's really the same idea, but we love the thought of the Lord tenderly collecting our tears in a bottle.
3. Matthew 11:28.
4. Hebrews 13:5 and Isaiah 43:1–2.
5. I especially love Isaiah 41:10.
6. Condensed and paraphrased from Barbara Johnson, *Fresh Elastic for Stretched Out Moms* (Grand Rapids, MI: Revel, 1985), 183.
7. Isaiah 61:3.
8. Adapted from Susannah Seton, Robert Taylor, and David Greer, comp., *Simple Pleasures* (Berkeley, CA: Conari Press, 1996), 174.

Chapter 16: Starting Your Day Right

1. C. S. Lewis, *Mere Christianity* (New York: Macmillan, 1978), chapter 30.
2. Linda Andersen, *Slices of Life,* quoted in Alice Gray, comp., *Morning Coffee and Time Alone: Bright Promise for a New Day* (Sisters, OR: Multnomah, 2000). Used by permission. Author of six books, including *Interludes* and *The Too Busy Book* (2004).
3. Leslie Sansone, "Come Walk with Me," *Woman's Day,* May 27, 2003, 58.
4. Dolley Carlson, *Gifts from the Heart* (Colorado Springs, CO: ChariotVictory, 1998), 41.

Chapter 17: Sleep Tight

1. Ruth Bell Graham, *Prodigals: And Those Who Love Them* (Grand Rapids, MI: Baker, 1999).
2. Ephesians 4:26, NASB.
3. Psalm 63:6–8, NIV.
4. Proverbs 3:24, NIV.
5. Psalm 121:4.

Chapter 18: So Much Beauty

1. Matthew 7:7, NIV.
2. Anne Morrow Lindbergh, *Gift from the Sea* (New York: Pantheon, 1955, 1975), 108.
3. 1 Samuel 16:16.